BoB DAV

LANDMARK COLLECTOR'S LIBRARY

THE REAL WOLSELEY:
ADDERLEY PARK WORKS
1901-1926

Norman Painting

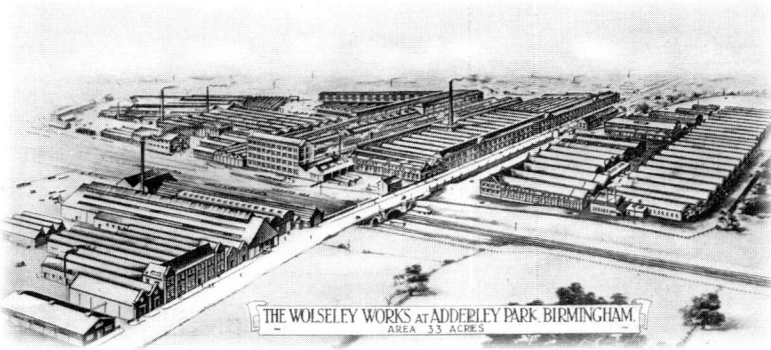

THE WOLSELEY WORKS at ADDERLEY PARK BIRMINGHAM.
AREA 33 ACRES

Published by

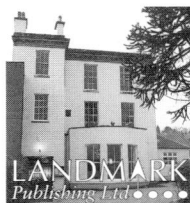

Landmark Publishing Ltd
Ashbourne Hall, Cokayne Ave, Ashbourne, Derbyshire DE6 1EJ England
Tel: (01335) 347349 Fax: (01335) 347303
e-mail: landmark@clara.net
web site: www.landmarkpublishing.co.uk

ISBN 1-84306-052-3

Print: Bookcraft, Midsomer Norton
Design: Mark Titterton
Cover: James Allsopp

Front Cover: An early Wolseley, photographed inside the works, pre – 1905.
Back Top Cover: The Wolseley stand at the Olympia Motor Show 1909.
Back Bottom Cover: The Stellite on Hodge Hill Common, 1913.

LANDMARK COLLECTOR'S LIBRARY

THE REAL WOLSELEY:
ADDERLEY PARK WORKS
1901-1926

Norman Painting

Landmark Publishing

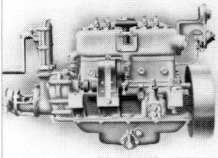

CONTENTS

ACKNOWLEDGEMENTS & REFERENCE

Whilst most of the photographs reproduced in this work are from the authors own archive collection of Wolseley sales and commemorative literature, acknowledgement is made to the British Motor Industry Heritage Trust, Heritage Motor Centre, Gaydon, for their kind permission to reproduce a number of Copyright images from their archive collection, individually identified with their captions. Some photographs are also included in this work by kind permission of Peter Seymour and John Wall, and a small number are also reproduced by courtesy of Birmingham Library Services.

Mr David Hill is acknowledged for his most valuable assistance whilst researching Wolseley submarine engines, and for supplying drawings, and for literature from "The Development of British Submarines from "Holland 1"(1901) to "Porpoise" (1930).

The staff of the Archives Department of Birmingham Central Library are also acknowledged for their patience and excellent service whilst the author researched 122 building drawings and other Wolseley items for this work, together with the staff of the Science and Technology Department, whilst studying patents, "The Autocar" 1895-1927, "Motor Traction" 1907-1920, and "The Great War & Armistice 1915-1919" for data concerning World War 1 aircraft. The staff of the Local History Department of the same establishment are also thanked for their service whilst carrying out general research into the Wolseley company, and the acquistion of certain photographs.

The staff of the Coventry Central Library, Local Studies & Reference Department, are also acknowledged for their assistance whilst researching the Bartleet Collection.

My thanks also to Durham University Library for access to "Vickers Sons & Maxim Ltd"., for information concerning the company's early manufacturies in Birmingham.

Valuable assistance was also provided by The Vintage Motor Cycle Club Ltd., Research Officer Mr. P.Heath.

I am also indebted to Mr B. Rowledge for access to archive material about his grandfather Arthur John Rowledge.

Thanks also to Dave Heritage for specific information about the boat "Ursula", and Mr. J.D.Siddeley and to Ken Hillier for his interesting contributions.

Other reference material included, "Wolseley - A Saga of the Motor Industry" by St. John. C. Nixon, "The Life of Lord Nuffield" by P.W.S. Andrews & Elizabeth Brunner, and "Out on a Wing" by Sir Miles Thomas.

Finally, my thanks to the late John Wall, a past employee of the Wolseley company, who kindly supplied material, such as personal reminiscences of past employees of the company, which led me into unknown pastures researching a motor car company when, at heart, I am a devoted commercial vehicle man!

"THE REAL WOLSELEY"
ADDERLEY PARK WORKS 1901-1926

INTRODUCTION

This book is not intended to be a comprehensive history of the Wolseley company, which continued to exist for many years after the period covered by this work, but it records the history of the company during its occupation of the Adderley Park Works, from its founding in 1901, to its financial collapse in 1926. The purpose of this publication is to illustrate briefly how the company developed the Adderley Park Works in parallel to the growth of the company and, through its patents and photographs, illustrate how Wolseley products were developed during the formative years of the company, through the war years and into the difficult post First World War years. Information concerning the actual factory buildings has been researched from original architects drawings submitted to Birmingham City Council for outline planning permission. Unfortunately, some drawings have been lost and planning applications for some buildings cannot be traced, so it has not been possible to date all the buildings accurately. The numbers of patents taken out by the company are all recorded in chronological order within the main body of the text, but some of these patents have been abandoned and copies are no longer available. However, for the technically minded reader/researcher it is well worth studying, in detail, the patents taken out by the company as they often reveal how their products were being developed, the innovative design work being done and also help to illustrate the great diversity of work being undertaken by the company whilst at the Adderley Park Works.

One cannot be anything but impressed by the diverse range of products made by Wolseley which included machine tools, motor cars, commercial vehicles, marine engines, industrial engines, railcar engines, aircraft engines, complete aircraft, airship engines and machinery, and all the wartime equipment like shells, gun mountings, armoured cars, staff cars, ambulances, Subsidy lorries, and gun sighting gear. Although Herbert Austin was instrumental in starting the company, the input of other engineers such as Arthur Rowledge, Alfred Remington and Edward Reeve cannot be underestimated and the loss of these men from the company obviously had an immense influence on the products of Wolseley, particularly in its difficult final years.

The overwhelming impression gained from researching this work was that the Wolseley company having risen from the very embryo of the motor industry to become the largest British motor car manufacturer, during the time scale covered by this work, was actually destroyed by the actions of its own parent, Vickers Ltd.

Norman Painting.
Birmingham. 1999.

DEDICATION

This book is dedicated to the late John Wall, who, like his father before him, worked at the Drews Lane factory of Wolseley Motors Ltd.

ALFRED ARNOLD REMINGTON, O.B.E., M.I.A.E. 1877-1922

After serving his apprenticeship at the Birmingham Kynoch company A.A.Remington became a Draughtsman with the Wolseley Sheep Shearing Machine Co.Ltd., transferring to the Wolseley Tool & Motor Car Co.Ltd., with Herbert Austin in 1901. In 1902 he was appointed Chief Draughtsman and, after Austin's departure in 1905, became Chief Designer for the company until about 1907 when he became Chief Engineer, a post he would hold until he left Wolseley in 1921.

In 1918/1919 Remington became President of the Institution of Automobile Engineers and was awarded the O.B.E., for his contribution to the Air Board during the First World War. Although Herbert Austin is always the first name historians associate with the Wolseley company, it was the brilliant talent of Remington leading their design team who engineered the world renowned Wolseley products long after Austin's resignation from the company but, hopefully, this brief work will be a fitting tribute to this very distinguished engineer.

(Photograph Courtsey of Birmingham Library Services)

ARTHUR JOHN ROWLEDGE M.B.E., F.R.S., F.R.A.S.1876-1957 *(Photographed much later in his life)*

Born in Peterborough, Rowledge served an apprenticeship with Barford & Perkins, after which he was employed as a draughtsman in London with the American printing machine makers R.Hoe & Co. In 1901 he joined the motor car makers D.Napier & Sons as a designer, during which time a Napier car won the Gordon Bennett road race. Soon after joining the Wolseley Tool & Motor Car Co.Ltd., in 1905 as Chief Draughtsman and later as Chief Designer, he married the daughter of H.H.Blincko, Esq. During his nine year stay with Wolseley he, together with Remington, was responsible for the design and development of motor car suspension, aero engines and motor car engines, including the cylinder head design of the little "Stellite" motor car. Leaving Wolseley at the end of 1913 Rowledge returned to Napier as Chief Draughtsman and later as Chief Designer, where he designed the 12 cylinder, triple bank, "Lion" aero engine which succeeded in holding no less than 24 British records for speed, duration and load carrying. In 1921 he joined Rolls-Royce Limited as Chief Assistant to Mr.F.H.Royce, where he designed the "Condor ", "Kestrel" and "Buzzard" aero engines, the latter becoming the basis for the engine which powered the 1929 and 1931 Schneider Trophy winning Supermarine aircraft. The need for a more compact engine led Rowledge into designing a V12 unit which eventually became the famous "Merlin" engine of World War 2.

JOHN DAVENPORT SIDDELEY C.B.E.

Siddeley appears to have started his life in industry with two of Coventry's largest cycle making companies and had been Managing Director of the Clipper Tyre Company in 1900 when he took part in the Thousand Miles Trial. About 1901 he became the British agent for Peugeot cars, and is believed to have sold some of these under his own name as a precursor to setting up The Siddeley Autocar Company in 1903, with cars designed by Wolseley and made in their Crayford Works. In 1905 Wolseley acquired the Siddeley motor car business and installed Siddeley himself as Sales Manager of Wolseley. Siddeley was exceedingly ambitious and signs of friction between Austin and Siddeley soon materialized in the form of Austin's resignation. Siddeley then became General Manager of Wolseley and soon had his name on company products, almost to the point of eclipsing the Wolseley name itself. Resigning in 1909, following pressure from the Wolseley Board, he joined the Deasy Motor Car Manufacturing Co.Ltd., in Coventry and became Lord Kenilworth in 1937.

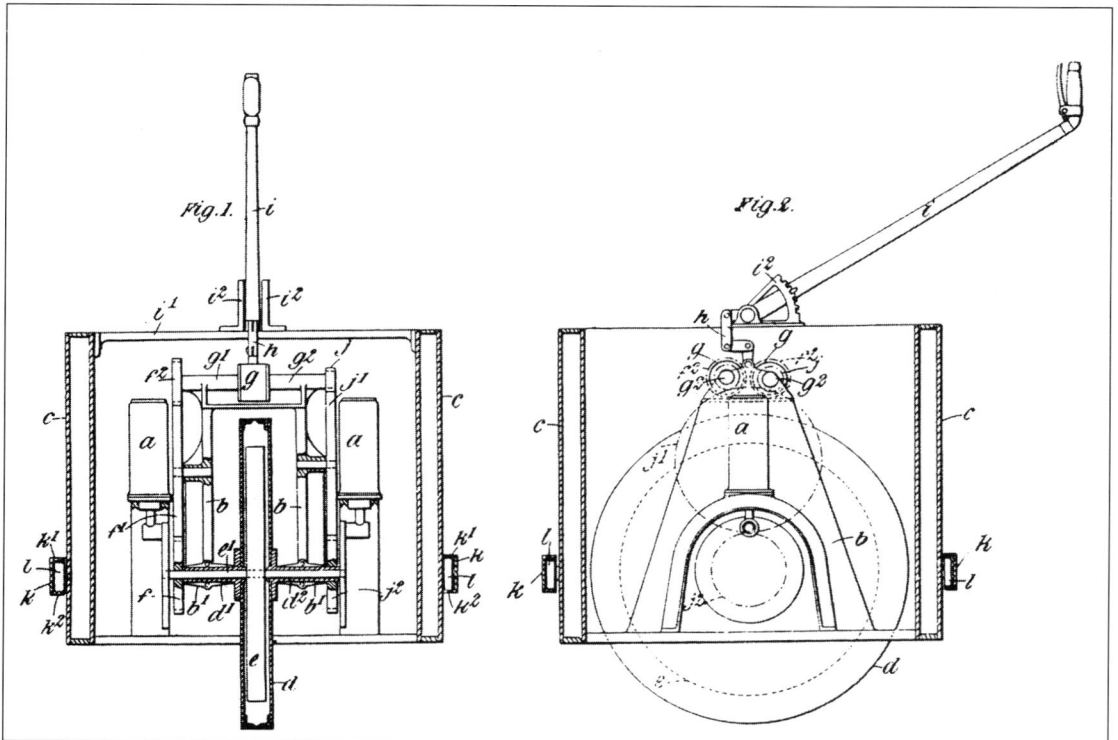

Fig.1.   Fig.2.

Frederick York Wolseley was born in County Dublin in 1837 and by 1868 had become manager of a sheep farm in Victoria, Australia. Wolseley was convinced that the shearing of sheep would be more efficiently accomplished by the use of mechanically operated shearing equipment and began experimenting with various designs on the sheep farm where he was employed. After a brief period in England he returned to Australia and in 1887 established the Wolseley Sheep-Shearing Machine Company Limited in Sydney. However, the products of the new company lacked the quality and reliability demanded of such equipment being used on isolated farms in the Australian Outback and the company was wound up about 1888.

Herbert Austin was born in Little Missenden, Bucks., and served an apprenticeship with the Great Northern Railway Company before going out to Australia in 1884 to work for an engineering company in North Melbourne. Moving from job to job Austin eventually became Manager of a small firm which was supplying parts to the Wolseley Sheep-Shearing Machine Company and was instrumental in improving the design and manufacture of sheep shearing equipment, taking out several patents connected with the work.

Frederick Wolseley returned to England and decided to wind up his Australian company and start a new company, with the same name, at 58½ Broad Street, Birmingham. The new company purchased the assets of the old Australian company for £141,665.

Austin, meantime, had continued to supply parts for the sheep shearing equipment and upon his return to England in 1893 the Wolseley Sheep-Shearing Machine Company Limited purchased all Austin's patents relating to sheep shearing equipment and Austin joined the company in Broad Street initially as an Inspector.

The Broad Street works, near Cumberland Street in Birmingham was situated somewhat inconspicuously between William Jones the Hairdresser and Mrs Tate Philpott's Dress Cutting Establishment, but in 1895 the company moved to larger premises in Alma Street, Aston, the factory being aptly named Sydney Works. As well as shearing equipment the company also manufactured machine tools and parts for the cycle industry including, it is believed, complete cycles. Austin, now Works Manager, however, was already taking more than a passing interest in a new form of transport being developed on the Continent, the motor car, and despite lacking any interest or financial assistance from the company he designed and built his first motor car at the Alma Street works in 1895.

His first car closely resembled the French Bollee car and was a three wheeled design where the driver sat between the two front steerable wheels and the 2 h.p. twin cylinder air cooled horizontally opposed petrol engine drove the single rear wheel via a three speed gearbox and chain drive. The single passenger seat was positioned above the rear wheel and illustrations of this car show the seat facing to the rear and alternatively, to the side with the passengers feet alongside the engine. Steering was effected by a tiller operating on the Ackermann principle and braking was via a rocking bar across the drivers footboard which actuated rods to an externally contracting brake on a 9" diameter drum on the rear wheel. This diminutive motor car was not offered for sale to the public as it was

PHOTOGRAPH

Herbert Austin's first motor car built in 1895 could more accurately be described as a motor tricycle. Powered by a two cylinder horizontal engine of about 2 h.p. this diminutive motor car could only carry one passenger. Tiller steering gear operated on the front wheels and the passenger seat is shown in some pictures fitted transversely above the rear driving wheel, in a position allowing the passenger to converse more easily with the driver!

ILLUSTRATION

This device patented on 25th August, 1896, patent number 18783, was basically a power pack in the form of a motorised wheel to enable a horse propelled vehicle to be easily converted to a motorised vehicle. The power pack was simply attached to the front axle of the horse drawn carriage by rearward facing arms extending from the sides of the engine casing, rather like the shafts which would have been used to attach a horse to the carriage.

The casing not only supported the engine, transmission and driving wheel, but also acted as a vessel to hold the engine coolant and fuel. Transmission was via the simple forward and reverse mechansim described in Austin's patent number 20401 and the extended tiller was designed to steer the vehicle. However, in practice, this would probably not have worked very well as it would have required considerable effort on the part of the driver to steer such a contraption effectively.

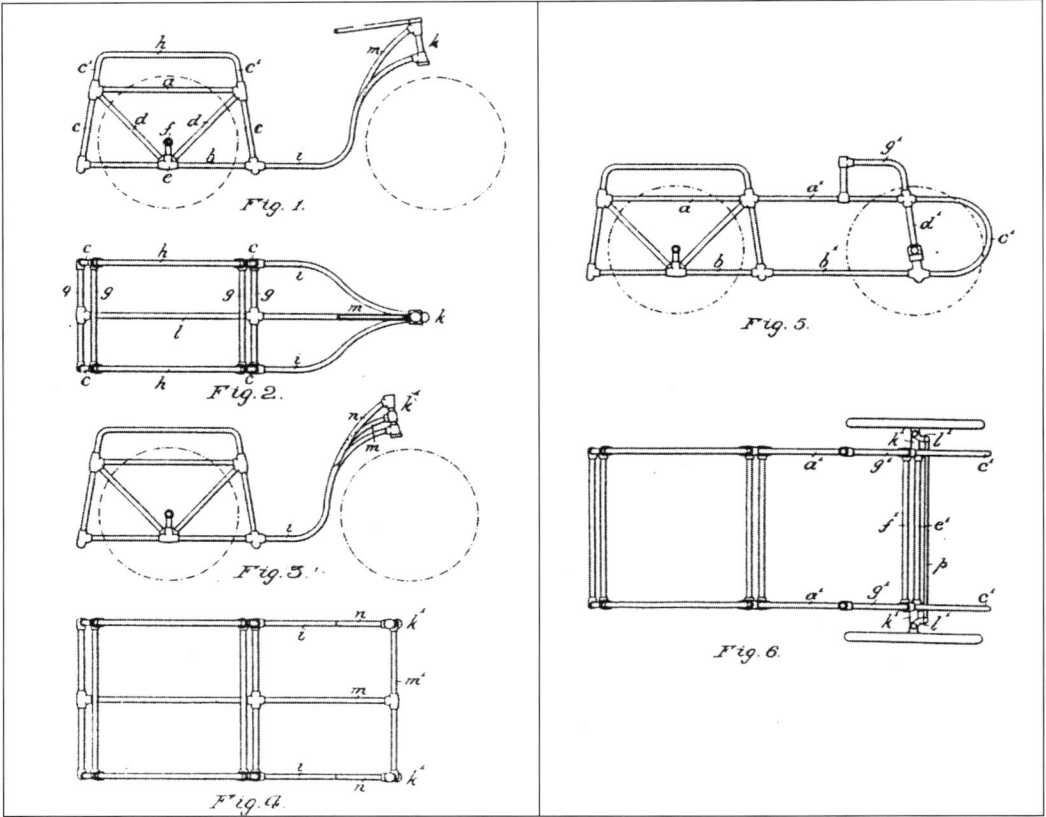

Fig. 1.

Fig. 2.

Fig. 3.

Fig. 4.

Fig. 5.

Fig. 6.

feared that the design was so like the Bollee that it would infringe their patents and it was used only for experimental purposes.

In 1895 Austin applied for two patents, numbers 20400 and 20401, which dealt with motor vehicles and driving gear for mechanical carriages, the latter dealing more specifically with a simple forward and reverse mechanism.

In 1896 Birmingham was being described in the motoring press as "an island isolated from the Autocar" and where an incident such as described now made headline news.

Exciting Runaway in Birmingham

"An extraordinary scene was witnessed at Moseley, a suburb of Birmingham, last night. Dr.Carters brougham was returning from a reception given by Mr. Chamberlain at Highbury, when his horse took fright and ran into a cab. The cabhorse also galloped off, and the pair ran furiously abreast for a mile and a half. Eventually, the cabhorse collided with a vehicle and was killed, and the brougham was smashed against a steam tram."

This was followed in February 1896 by a report of a Mr. Leon L'Hollier (a partner in the Anglo French Motor Carriage Company of Digbeth, Birmingham) who, after driving a motor car on the Stratford Road, was fined when he " unlawfully did not, while the locomotive was in motion on the said highway, have a person on foot preceding the said locomotive by at least 20 yards."

It is difficult to imagine Birmingham now without motor vehicles, but practically every new sighting of a motor car or motor bicycle on the streets of Birmingham in those days was reported in the motoring press and this helps to put into perspective the era in which Austin and other designers were developing their first motor cars in Britain.

Austin's second car built in 1896 could more accurately be described as a motorised tricycle, so light was its construction and appearance. The design was almost the reverse of Austin's first car in as much as it featured a single wheel at the front, steered by a tiller, with two driven wheels at the rear. The driver now sat behind the front wheel with the passenger still facing to the rear, but the engine was now fully enclosed by the simple bodywork which formed a box for the two seats. The engine was a twin cylinder water cooled unit and drive was via an epicyclic gear train.

Problems with the second car appear to have been manifest and Austin abandoned the engine and transmission designs in favour of a single cylinder engine with an air cooled cylinder head and water cooled cylinder block which had a bore of 4" diameter and stroke of 4.9375" and belt driven transmission. Only two speeds were provided in the modified design of 1897, but the braking system now consisted of a footbrake actuating expanding shoes within rims attached to the rear wheels and a handbrake operating separate shoes within the same wheel rims. The car also featured independent suspension of the rear wheels.

The improvements to the design of car number two obviously impressed the Directors of the Wolseley Sheep Shearing Machine Co.Ltd., as a sales brochure was printed and cars offered for sale to the general public, priced at £110 to carry two people and £150 to carry four people. (Although sales brochures were published, it is believed that no cars of this design were actually sold) The main framework for both cars was of steel tubing and Austin applied for

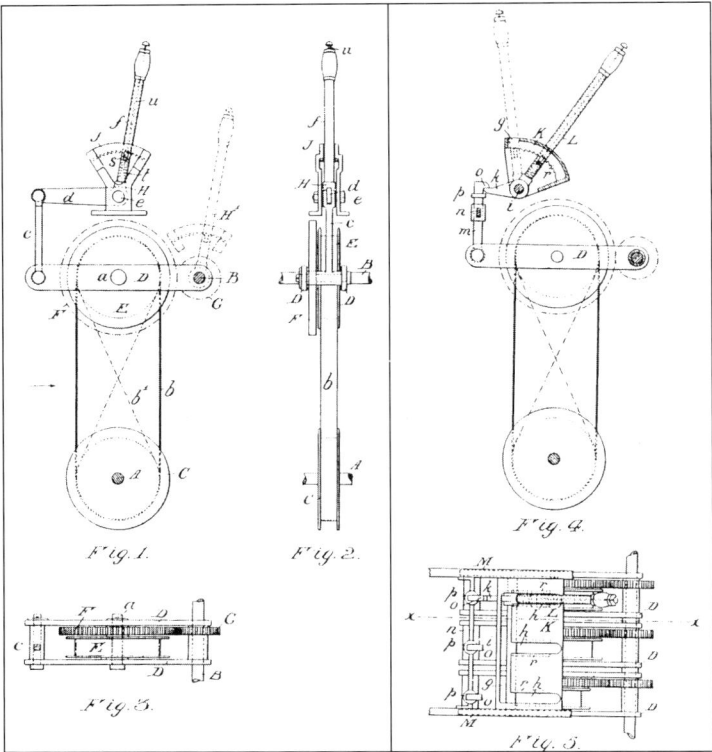

Fig. 1. *Fig. 2.* *Fig. 4.*

Fig. 3.

Fig. 5.

ILLUSTRATION

These drawings from Austin's patent number 104, dated 2nd January, 1897, illustrate means by which arrangements of levers, ratchets, belts and pulleys could be used to control the starting and stopping, changes of speed and change in the direction of travel of a motor car.

A pulley driven directly by the engine could be connected to, or disengaged from a similar pulley arranged to drive the wheels of the motor car by slackening the drive belt between them using a hand operated lever to slacken, or tighten the belt to provide a simple clutch device. A similar arrangement, but using pulleys of different diameters, could also be employed to facilitate the acquisition of different speeds, or ratios, to the driven wheels and, an arrangement of two pulleys with a crossed belt between them and also controlled by a hand lever could be used to select either forward, or reverse motion. Grouping these devices together, as shown in Figure 4, provided a clutch, 2 speeds and a reverse mechanism.

a patent, number 12394, to cover their designs in 1896. Other patents applied for in the same year included 18783 which covered the design of a motorised wheel which bolted between the front wheels of a carriage, 23526 and 28135, covering wheel hubs and motor car engines respectively. In 1897 Austin applied for two more patents, numbers 104 and 1018, both covering improvements to driving gear for motor vehicles.

Frederick York Wolseley died in January 1899, in Surrey, never having seen a motor car bearing his name, but development work continued and the Wolseley company announced their first four wheeled car late in 1899. The "Wolseley Voiturette", priced at £270, was powered by a single cylinder water cooled horizontal engine with a bore of 4.5" diameter and stroke of 5" and developing about 5 h.p. A three speed gearbox was now featured with a 'gate change' and belt drive from the engine to a countershaft, then via chains to the rear wheels. Tiller steering was still retained but operated a worm and worm wheel steering box on the front axle. In a trial consisting of driving the car from Birmingham to Coventry and back plus a hill climb of the notorious Mucklow Hill in Halesowen the car covered the 38 miles in 4 hours 58 minutes and climbed Mucklow Hill in a little over 11 minutes, earning itself a Silver Medal in the process.

A total of seven patents were applied for in 1898, 4053, 19195, 20082, 20083, 20765, 23288 and 26206, covering such subjects as speed gears, engines and carburettors.

Since about 1897 the Alma Street works had also been able to offer components to the cycle trade and casting facilities to the motor trade, but did not manufacture complete cycles. The machinery side of the business was also expanding and they exhibited an automatic screw cutting machine and a disc grinding machine at the Stanley Cycle Show held in London in November 1900.

A 3 h.p. "Wolseley Voiturette", driven by Herbert Austin, took part in the 1900 Thousand Miles Trial organized by the Automobile Club of Great Britain and Ireland, entry number 40, and was awarded a £10 prize by 'The Daily Mail' newspaper and a Silver Medal from the Automobile Club de France. This vehicle, which was now priced at £225, was exhibited later in the year at the Bingley Hall, Broad Street in Birmingham, close to the site of the original sheepshearing machine company.

Experience from the Thousand Miles Trial led to the introduction of an improved model announced in June 1900 which also featured a conventional steering wheel for the first time on a Wolseley car. Orders for the "Wolseley Voiturette" flooded in to the Alma Street works and it was soon apparent that the factory would not be able to cope with production of these cars as well as all the other products being manufactured there.

A new company was formed called the Wolseley Tool & Motor Car Company Limited and premises were acquired at Adderley Park under the auspices of Vickers Sons & Maxim Ltd., who paid the Wolseley Sheep Shearing Machine Co.Ltd., £12,400 in cash and 67 five per cent. second debentures of £100 each for the motor car side of their business.

Herbert Austin was appointed Manager and Alfred Remington also transferred from the sheep shearing business to Adderley Park as a draughtsman and the development of new cars commenced in March 1901.

PHOTOGRAPH

The first four wheeled motor car, with tiller steering, which competed in the Thousand Mile Trial of 1900 driven by Herbert Austin and which gained First Prize in its class and 10% of the total prize money. This car was preserved by the company, although it is minus its drive chain here, and is now part of the Heritage Collection of motor cars at Gaydon in Warwickshire.

The Trial consisted of a circuitous route from London to Edinburgh and back and included a series of one day exhibitions where the 84 entrants were to be put on show in Bristol, Birmingham, Manchester, Edinburgh, Newcastle on Tyne, Leeds and Sheffield, and with a final 7 day exhibition at Crystal Palace in London. The Trial was not a race, but was intended to prove the reliability and durability of these early motor cars whilst trying to maintain speeds within the general speed limits of the period, 12 m.p.h. in England and 10 m.p.h. in Scotland.

Petrol for cars taking part had to be ordered well in advance from Agents en route, at prices from 1s-2d to 2s-0d per gallon, the cheapest petrol being supplied by the Anglo American Oil Company. A second Wolseley car, a 4 seater 8 h.p. Carriage, entry number 53, also took part, but was withdrawn after completing just a few of the early sections. However, the "Voiturette" completed the whole course with average speeds of 12 m.p.h. on twelve of the thirteen sections, falling to 10 m.p.h. on the Carlisle to Edinburgh section where it suffered several punctures which delayed the car for about one hour. A short speed trial was held over a one mile course on the Duke of Portland's estate at Welbeck where the Wolseley averaged 22.81 m.p.h.

The official programme for the Trial even included brief details of hotels around the route where competitors could stay overnight, or take meals. Interestingly, The Grand Hotel in Colmore Row, Birmingham was listed as having accommodation for 50 guests and 10 valets, with single bedrooms from 5s-0d per night, dinner from 2s-6d to 5s-0d, luncheon from 2s-0d to 3s-0d and breakfast for 2s-0d or 2s-6d.!!

ARDEN ROAD

BROWN, MARSHALLS & CO. LTD.
Railway Carriage & Waggon Builders.

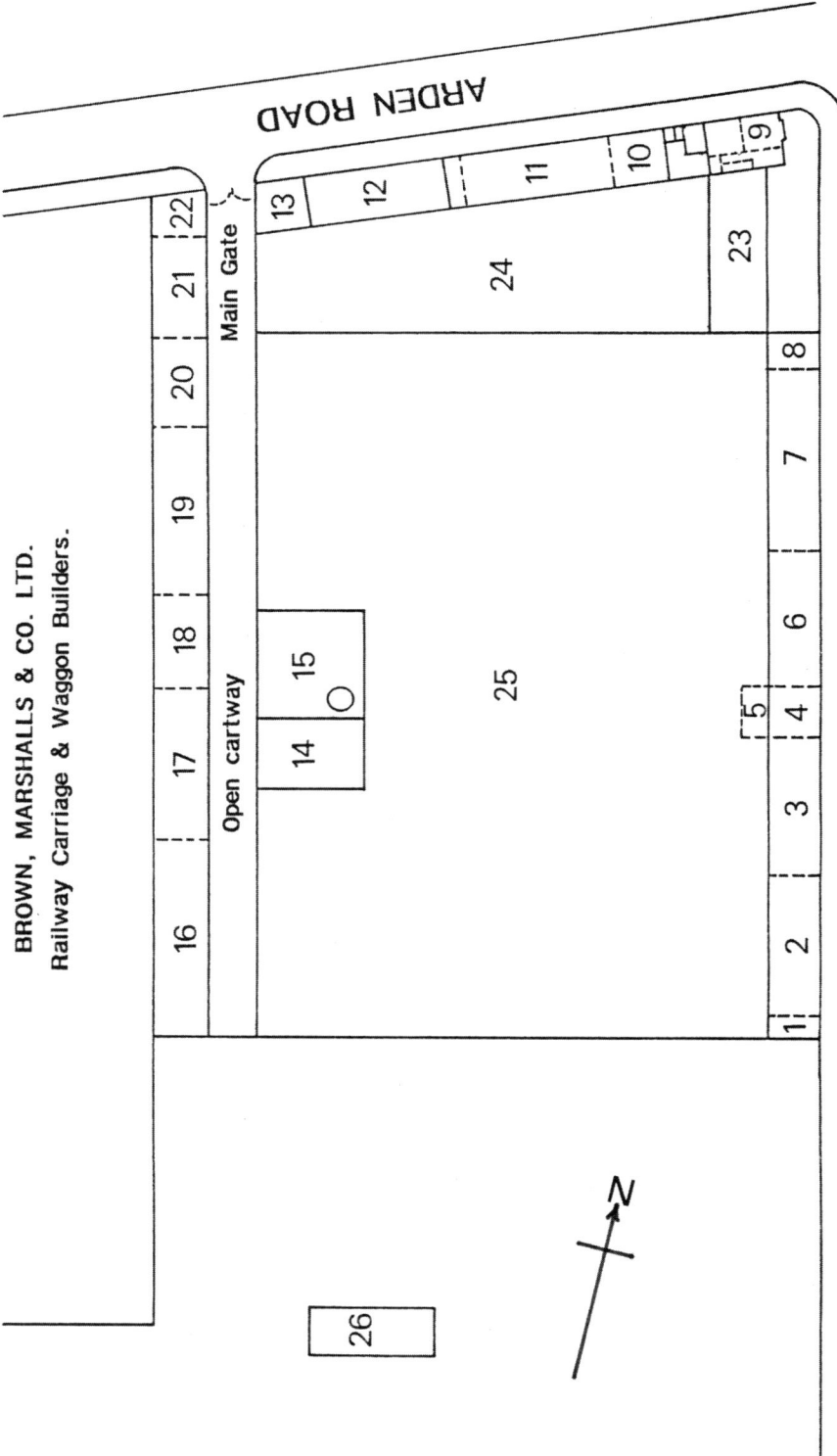

Main Gate

Open cartway

BORDESLEY GREEN ROAD

STARLEY BROTHERS & WESTWOOD LTD.
1897

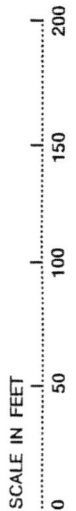

SCALE IN FEET

0   50   100   150   200

N

PLAN OF PREMISES ERECTED IN 1897 BY STARLEY BROTHERS & WESTWOOD LIMITED AND USED FROM 1901 TO HOUSE THE WOLSELEY TOOL & MOTOR CAR COMPANY LIMITED.

(Starley Brothers & Westwood had been formed in 1896 when William Starley joined The Westwood Manufacturing Company, the joint venture having a capital of £130,000. The company proved to be a complete failure and shortly after a shareholders meeting in 1899, held at the Adderley Park works, the company was wound up with the ordinary shareholders losing everything. Manufacture of the products being made at the works was then transferred to the Ariel works in Selly Oak, Birmingham. William Starley had also been involved in another failure which was wound up in 1898, Starley Brothers (Russia) Ltd., which lost every penny of its £100,000 capital.)

1. Girls Toilet, 9ft 7ins by 20ft.
2. Warehouse & General Stores, 59ft 3ins by 20ft.
3. Packing & Stores for wheel rims, 59ft 3ins by 20ft.
4. Main Office Entrance, 19ft 5ins by 20ft with direct access to Main Works Building.
5. Workshop Foremans Office.
6. Packing & Stores for forks, 59ft 3ins by 20ft.
7. Rough Stores for tubes, 79ft 7ins by 20ft.
8. Loading Dock, 16ft by 20ft.
9. House with ground floor Living Room, Sitting Room, Scullery, Larder, outside Toilet and Coal House and upstairs, two Bedrooms and a Bathroom.
10. Kitchens on ground floor and upper floor, 20ft by 20ft.
11. Mens Mess Room on ground floor, 60ft by 20ft and Girls Mess Room on upper floor.
12. Carpenters Shop, 55ft by 20ft. Single storey building.
13. Toilets, 16ft by 20ft.
14. Boiler House, 30ft by 43ft.
15. Muffles, 47ft 8ins by 43ft with chimney stack for Boiler House.
16. Enamelling Shop, 73ft 6ins by 22ft.
17. Smiths Shop, 60ft by 22ft.
18. Joint Brazing Shop, 36ft by 22ft.
19. Fork & Rim Brazing Shop, 70ft by 22ft.
20. Pickling Shop, 36ft by 22ft.
21. Loading Shop, 40ft by 22ft.
22. Time Office, 15ft 3ins by 22ft.
23. Open Yard, 67ft by 22ft.
24. Covered Yard.
25. Main Works.
26. L.N.W.R. Railway Cottages.

ADDERLEY PARK WORKS

The factory acquired by the Wolseley Tool & Motor Car Company Limited had been built in 1897 by Starley Brothers & Westwood Ltd., manufacturers to the cycle trade, at the corner of Bordesley Green Road and Arden Road. Plans for the building show a first floor office for Mr. Westwood, but the Starley brothers appear to have been in name only, as no office accomodation was provided for them.

The works, designed by Frederick Lloyd of New Street, Birmingham, comprised an imposing two storey building built parallel to the Bordesley Green Road which measured 300 feet long by 22 feet wide, built from bricks made locally at the nearby Adderley Park Brick Works, Bordesley Green Road, one of three such works in the area, the others being the Parkfield Brick Company and the Britannia Brick Works, and had originally housed a Warehouse, Stores and Loading Bay on the ground floor and offices on the first floor which included a Board Room 38 feet long by 16 feet wide.

At the corner of Bordesley Green Road and Arden Road was a two bedroomed house integral with the works buildings and built, presumably, to house a Caretaker or Works Manager, for the works. Behind the house, running parallel to Arden Road, was a two storey building which had housed separate Mess Rooms for men and women, each with separate entrances from Arden Road, together with a single storey building which had been used as a Carpenters Shop, this part of the works measuring 160 feet long by 22 feet wide.

To the rear of the office block was the single storey Main Works area, 300 feet by 208 feet, built in 15 bays each 20 feet wide, with its floor level about 6 feet lower than the ground floor of the offices and which included a Boiler House and Muffles and an underground storage tank for rain water collected from the roof of the building. A 20 feet wide open cartway, the gateway to which formed the Main Works Entrance in Arden Road, separated the main works building from a long single storey building 330 feet long by 22 feet wide which had originally housed workshops for Frame Brazing, Fork & Rim Brazing, Pickling, Enamelling and a Time Office adjacent to the main entrance.

The works, when originally taken over by the company at a cost of £31,545, covered just over 2 acres on a 3½ acres site, but this was to alter rapidly as demand for motor cars and other products increased and the factory was expanded to cope with the introduction of more and more models.

Initially the Coppersmiths Shop, Foundry, Smithy's and Forging Shop were all located in the out buildings separated from the main works. The Coppersmiths Shop assembled radiators and the Forging Shop, which had four hearths and a steam hammer, forged parts such as brake levers, change speed levers and front and rear axles.

The Machine Shop situated in the main works area contained several machine tools made by the company itself, plus machines such as an 18 feet planer made by Gray & Co., of Cincinnati, and lathes, boring machines and capstan lathes made by British companies. By 1902 420 machine tools had been installed in the machine shop alone, plus another 80 machines of various kinds in other departments of the works. To power all this machinery a huge steam driven dynamo was installed to provide electricity for the 13

ARDEN ROAD

Main Gate

Open cartway

BROWN, MARSHALLS & CO. LTD.
Railway Carriage & Waggon Builders.

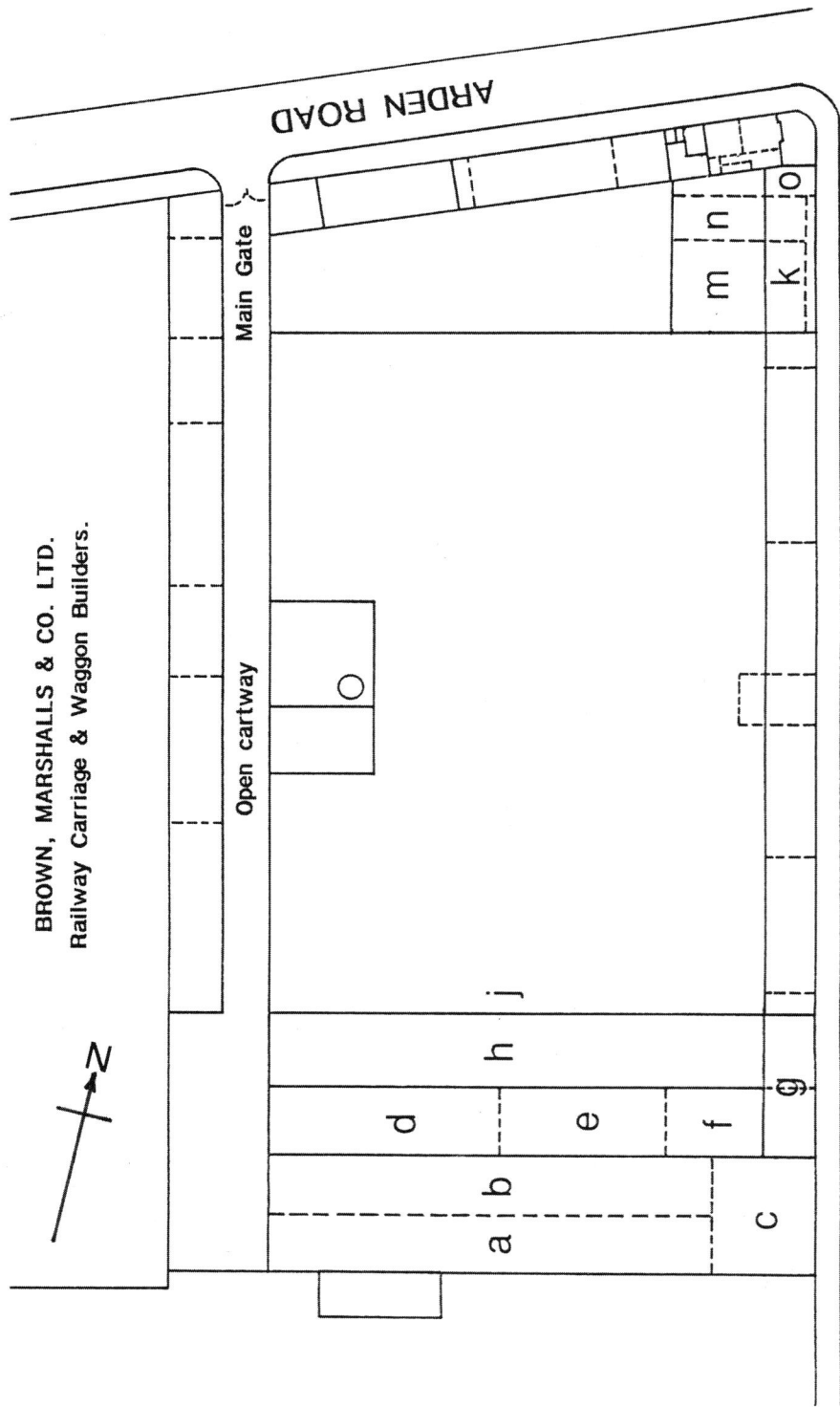

N

d

a b

c

h j

e

f

g

m n

k o

SCALE IN FEET

0   50   100   150   200

BORDESLEY GREEN ROAD

WOLSELEY TOOL & MOTOR CAR COMPANY LIMITED
FACTORY EXPANSION – 1902 & 1903

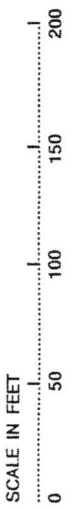

a. Heavy Iron Foundry, 25ft 6ins by 187ft. Built up to the railway cottages which then formed the south boundary of the site.

b. Light Iron Foundry, 25ft 6ins by 187ft.

c. Brass Foundry 43ft by 51ft.

d. Body Shop, 30ft by 100ft.

e. Woodworking Machine Shop, 30ft by 70ft.

f. Pattern Making Shop, 30ft by 63ft.

g. Two storey high extension to Main Offices, 64ft 6ins by 22ft. The Drawing Office was on the first floor of this new extension.

h. New Erecting Shop, 30ft by 230ft. The end of this shop and the Pattern Making Shop extended under the office extension (g).

j. Existing Erection Shop.

The iron foundries were equipped with two cupolas capable of producing up to 10 tons of molten metal per hour, and sand for the moulds was prepared in a 5ft diameter marl mill.

The aluminium foundry had a total of six crucible furnaces with a capacity of 1 ton per day. Aluminium castings included a 74lbs 10 h.p. engine casing and a 93lbs gearbox casing.

FACTORY EXPANSION - 1903

k. Two Storey extension of Main Office building, 74ft by 22ft with Stores on ground floor having access to Bordesley Green Road and to the area which had been a covered yard prior to this extension being built.

m. The first floor of the new office extension was extended rearwards 40ft to provide a Paint Shop 56ft by 40ft and Trimming Shop.

n. Trimming Shop, 56ft by 20ft.

o. Staff Mess Room on ground floor measuring 13ft by 20ft.

electric motors, made by another Vickers company, which drove the overhead lineshafts, the motors having a total output of 350 h.p.

The Engine Assembly and Test Shop was also located in the main works with engines being run at full power, at 750 r.p.m., for at least one hour before being fitted into chassis.

Chassis erection also took place in this building and upon completion 'slave' bodies would be fitted and the cars road tested for 100 miles. Only after being passed off as satisfactory would the chassis be washed down and fitted with the body requested by the prospective owner. The Paint Shop too was located in this building, but partitioned off from other working areas and built with tiled walls and floor to enable it to be kept spotlessly clean.

By May 1901 the company had published its first catalogue of motor cars which included 5 h.p. and 10 h.p. horizontal engined models available with 'Phaeton' or 'Tonneau' bodywork and also with the option of solid tyres or pneumatic tyres, the prices ranging from £260 to £380. The belt drive between the engine and gearbox had been abandoned in favour of a more positive chain drive and a leather to metal cone type clutch introduced. Light delivery vans were also available and, somewhat surprisingly for a company just established, a racing car with a 20 h.p. four cylinder horizontal engine.

Austin applied for two new patents, also in May 1901, 9325 and 9539, dealing with a handbrake mechanism and a new design of gearbox where the gears could be partially pre- selected before the actual gearchange took place.

After making a loss of £5,429 in the first ten months of production the company rapidly went on to make a profit of £5,400 by December 1902.

It is not too difficult to imagine the size of the problems facing a company entering this completely new industry at the turn of the century when most of the components still required constant trial and experimental work to make them reliable and even new types of machine tools needed to be developed to manufacture components to extremely fine tolerances. The petrol engine itself was still largely an unknown quantity and design changes were constantly needed to keep it abreast of latest developments, added to which, transmissions and suspension design had to cope with rapidly changing engine power and road speeds and conditions and even the bodywork being carried over from the traditional carriage makers required considerable development to cope with motor car applications.

However, with the parent company, Vickers, heavily involved in supplying products for government contracts it was no surprise to find the fledgling Wolseley company already in the process of supplying motor cars to the War Office for Staff Officers and Scouting, together with vehicles specially adapted to carry generating sets for searchlights. The company was also involved in supplying engines for special locomotives for use in South African mines, being 2 cylinder units with a bore of 6ins diameter, stroke of 7ins, and producing 18 h.p. at 600 r.p.m. The locomotives were being supplied by another company, and were only 3ft 6ins high, of 18ins gauge, had a top speed of 20 m.p.h. and could haul 24,000 lbs.

February 1902 saw the first of many building applications by the company to enlarge the factory when plans were submitted to

LEFT: The top picture shows a 1902 10 h.p. Double Tonneau, priced at about £380. A similar car, but with solid tyres, owned by a gentleman in Weston-super-Mare was reported to be giving excellent service after covering 3,524 miles and using 241.5 gallons of petrol (an average of 14.59 m.p.g.) at a cost of £15-12s-6d, plus 16s-9d for grease and oil.

The lower picture shows an unusual looking machine which was an experimental fire appliance designed by a Captain Wells and supplied to the London County Council Metropolitan Fire Brigade in October 1903. The vehicle was powered by a 24 h.p. engine and the semi-trailer was originally part of a horse drawn appliance. The company also built a number of "First Aid" fire appliances for London in 1903, based upon 10 h.p. motor car chassis and fitted with simple pick-up type bodies. More conventional fire appliances were supplied to Glasgow and Birmingham and one Wolseley fire appliance was also supplied to the Christchurch Fire Brigade in New Zealand.

extend the two storey office building along the Bordesley Green Road by 64 feet 6 inches to provide additional Stores on the ground floor and a Drawing Office on the upper floor. The extension was built to match the design of the original building.

Additionally, a new single storey Erecting Shop, Pattern Shop, Wood Working Shop and Body Shop 60 feet by 200 feet were also built together with an Iron and Brass Foundry measuring 232 feet long by 51 feet wide alongside the Main Works on its south wall, the Foundry building extending to the pavement in Bordesley Green Road hard by the new office extension. The Foundry was equipped with a narrow gauge rail track system which enabled castings to be taken from the foundry direct to the machine shop established in the main works area of the factory and two cupolas gave the new foundry a capacity of up to 10 tons per hour. The new office and works buildings cost £8,000, but orders for cars stood at £120,000 and the company had received orders totalling £18,000 in just one week of 1902. This demand for cars meant increasing the workforce from just over 400 in February to 600 in March.

In February 1902, just one week before his ship was to sail to Africa, Cecil Rhodes ordered a 10 h.p. car. Unable to build a car at such short notice Wolseley contacted some of their customers whose cars were ready and waiting at the works for delivery and found one obliging gentleman who agreed to let his new car go to Mr. Rhodes whilst he had to return to the waiting list.(Demand for the 10 h.p. model was so great that orders were already extending into the early months of 1903) Cecil Rhodes could not have enjoyed his car for long, as he died on March 26th shortly after reaching Muizenburg in the Cape and was buried in the Matopo Hills.

Austin applied for six patents in 1902, numbers 260, 261, 10002, 20444, 20445 and 24975, which covered such diverse subjects as motor car bodies, differential gearing, sparking plugs and electrical wire terminals.

The range of motor cars had now been extended to cover a 5 h.p. model with a single cylinder engine; 7½ h.p. with a twin cylinder engine having a bore and stroke of 4" and three speed gearbox; 10 h.p. with twin cylinder engine and three speed gearbox; 20 h.p.

RIGHT: A tractor built in 1904 and powered by a two cylinder 24 h.p. horizontal petrol engine. The 'chimney' was, in fact, the exhaust pipe. There appears to be no form of suspension at the front axle which was probably centrally pivoted and, with the steering actuated by a small steering wheel and chains, followed traction engine practice of this period. Tractors similar to this were supplied for trials to the War Office in 1906, possibly for use as field artillery tractors, but were powered by 30 h.p. 4 cylinder engines which ran on paraffin. (Photograph Courtesy of Birmingham Library Services.)

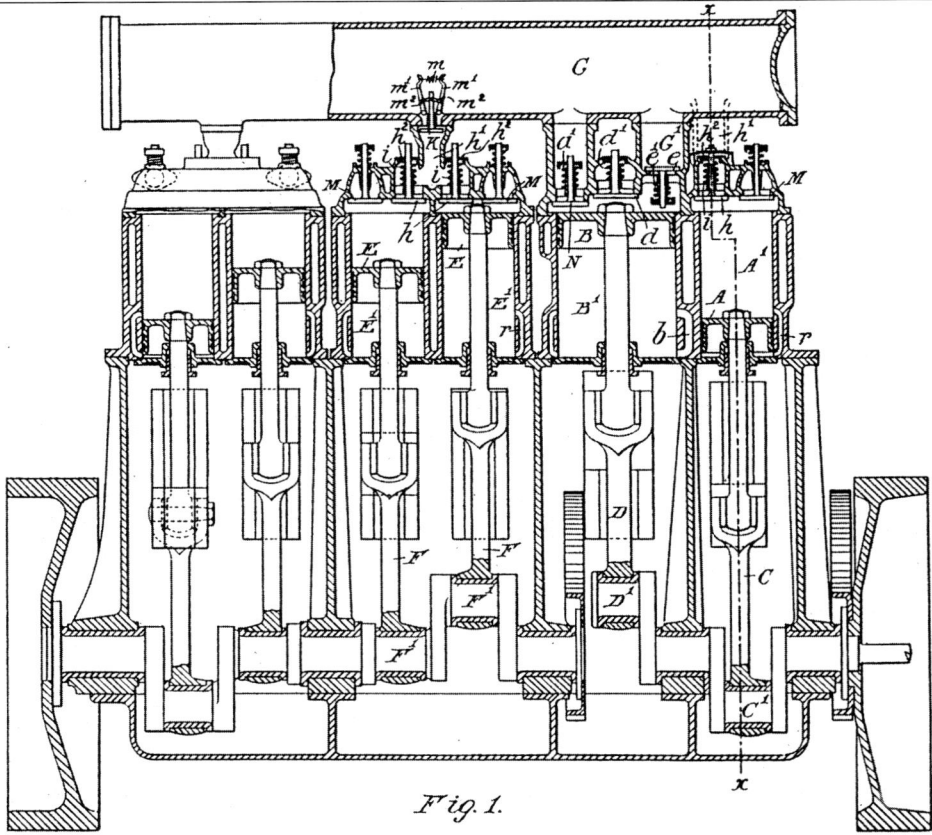

Fig. 1.

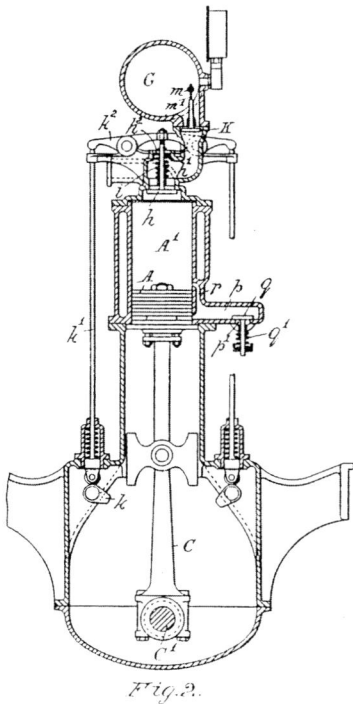

Fig. 2.

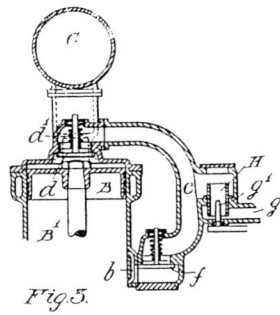

Fig. 5.

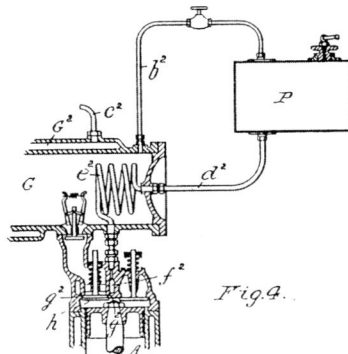

Fig. 4.

PATENT NUMBER 20342
DATED 9th OCTOBER, 1905

At first glance one would be forgiven for thinking that this patent dealt with the design of a six cylinder engine. However, with a flywheel at each end of the crankshaft this is quite obviously something very different and, in fact, the patent deals with the design of a two stroke engine having four cylinders shown on the left of the diagram (Figure 1) and a single cylinder two stroke engine driving a single cylinder pump on the right of the diagram, all in one cylinder block casting. There are two separate crank-shafts, one with three journals for the four cylinder engine and one with two journals for the single cylinder engine and pump. The construction of this engine would indicate that it was intended for marine or industrial use and would have been of quite substantial proportions.

The engine would be started using the single cylinder engine which drove the pump. The pump was used to compress a fuel/air mixture drawn into the pump via a simple form of carburettor and fill the large tubular reservoir mounted longitudinally on top of the engine. This engine design has been referred to as a Super Brayton, or semi-diesel engine, as the pre-compressed air/fuel was admitted into the cylinder in a compression ignitable form. The tubular reservoir was of sufficient proportions "to prevent an explosion" and was fitted with safety valves which closed instantly if one of the cylinders back fired. The valve gear design also allowed the four cylinder propulsion engine to be run in reverse if so desired.

Figure 2 shows a cross section through one of the working cylinders of the main propulsion engine and Figure 3 shows a small cross section through the single cylinder pump and how it was supplied with fuel via the carburettor (H). Figure 4 shows an alternative means of introducing fuel into the tubular reservoir by injecting fuel through a pressurised tank (P).

The patent was taken out by Alfred Remington. There are references in some Wolseley literature that a 6 cylinder submarine engine had been built at the works, but no other details have ever come to light. However, could this 6 cylinder engine actually have been an engine built to this patent? Externally it would have looked like a conventional engine, other than having two flywheels, and the single cylinder engine/air pump would most certainly have been advantageous in a submarine to start up the main 4 cylinder engine.

with four cylinder engine, all these being horizontal engines with a bore of 4½" diameter and stroke of 5" and featuring four speed gearboxes. Additionally, a 30 h.p. racing car was also being offered fitted with a four cylinder horizontal engine with 5" diameter bore and 5" stroke, all the models in the 1902 range having chain final drive. The racing car was entered in various races and speed trials during 1902 including the Paris-Vienna race where it broke its crankshaft half way through the race. In a speed trial held at Welbeck Park the car covered the flying kilometre in 51.3 seconds at a speed of 43.66 m.p.h.

The year 1903 did not start well for the company as a fire in the Paint Shop, on Friday 23rd January, resulted in smoke and water damage to about 20 cars, several of which were in the process of being prepared for the forthcoming Crystal Palace Show.

In March the company was sued by a Mrs Wainwright of Tonbridge after her horse was involved in an accident with a Wolseley works car during the Automobile Club Trials. The horse broke a leg and had to be shot, but Mrs Wainwright won her case and was awarded £75.

Expansion of the factory continued in 1903 when a small Photographic Studio (it is believed that the company had a policy of photographing practically every motor car made, together with its new owner, or representative, before leaving the works) was added to the first floor of the main offices and built over the roof of the workshop to the rear of the main office building which itself was extended again, this time at the northern end. This latest extension added 74 feet of Stores to the two storey frontage of this building taking it up to the house built into the original works and to the rear built at first floor level the building was extended 40 feet to totally enclose the open yard to provide a Trimming Shop 20 feet by 56 feet and a Paint Shop 40 feet by 56 feet. A small Staff Mess Room was also provided at the north end of the new extension.

In 1903 Austin applied for nine patents, numbers 5101, 5720, 6461, 7535, 15801, 22225, 22226, 22305 and 22317, covering the design of engines, carburettors, carriage door latches and radiators. Patent number 22225 is of particular interest as it deals with the mounting of a twin cylinder vertical engine in a motor car chassis.

The car range for 1903 remained much the same as for the previous year the one notable exception being the racing car which now featured a 50 h.p. four cylinder horizontal engine with a bore of 6" diameter and stroke of 6½", a massive 11.97 litres capacity. Although entered in several competitions by private owners and works drivers the car appears not to have gained any awards and experimental work continued to develop an even more powerful car which would be competitive. One racing car was bought by a Lieutenant Mansfield Cumming R.N., the machine being powered by a four cylinder horizontal engine which developed full power at 900 r.p.m., had a four speed gearbox, 25 gallon fuel tank, a wheelbase of 8ft 9ins, front track of 4ft 6ins and weighed just under 1,000 kgs. In June Cummings took part in the Paris-Madrid Race where he covered one section of the route at an average of 62.13 m.p.h. and was timed on another section at a maximum of 68.66 m.p.h.

Two notable orders in 1903 were for a 10 h.p. carriage, with enclosed passenger compartment, for H.R.H. Prince Louis of Battenberg and a 12 h.p. car of similar design ordered by the Czar

LEFT: (BMIHT photo) The Hardening Shop was located in the group of single storey buildings alongside the open cartway of the original works, probably in building '19' which had previously housed the Fork & Rim Brazing Shop. The windows to the right of the picture opened directly onto the open cartway. The most astonishing thing about this picture is that the gas fired ovens on the left had chimneys which exhausted into the workshop itself and the only ventilation provided was via the small windows to the right and a large trap door in the roof of the building, top centre.

ABOVE: (BMIHT photo). The Engine Erecting Shop was located in area '24' of the factory and was taken about 1904/6. The enormous engine under construction in the left foreground appears to be one of the 6 cylinder horizontal engines built for railcar use, as supplied to the Delaware & Hudson Railway Company and the Schenectady Company of New York. With a bore of 8½" diameter and stroke of 12" these 140 h.p. engines had a capacity of about 55 litres and, interestingly, two 4 cylinder engines of similar size/configuration are also under construction in this picture.

of Russia as a wedding gift for Princess Alice of Battenberg who was marrying Prince Andreas of Greece. The latter car, which had seats for five passengers, plus the driver, was finished in dark blue morocco leather with silver fittings.

In April the parent company, Vickers Sons & Maxim Ltd., announced its intention to build a cheap Wolseley at a factory in Crayford, Kent, which occupied about 25 acres. The 6 h.p. Voiturette had a chassis frame formed out of a single piece of channel section steel, joined at the front of the frame by a simple crossmember, was powered by a single cylinder horizontal engine with a bore of 4.125" and stroke of 5 inches and with a speed range of 800 r.p.m.-1,000 r.p.m. A three speed gearbox drove the rear axle via a Renolds chain and gave the little 2 seater a top speed of 25 m.p.h. With a wheelbase of 5ft 6ins and track of 4ft 0in the unladen weight was 8½ cwts and cost £175. Despite being built in Kent, at a rate of about 20 cars per week, Vickers pointed out that these new cars were to be built under the supervision of Herbert Austin.

The company started to enter other fields of interest and in March 1903 supplied two massive 80 h.p. four cylinder engines to the North Eastern Railway Company for use in motor railway coaches. The engines had a bore of 8½ inches diameter and stroke of 10 inches, giving a total capacity of 37 litres, consumed petrol at the rate of about 10 gallons per hour and had a speed range of 420 r.p.m. to 480 r.p.m. The railcars carried 25 passengers, weighed 35 tons were capable of 40 m.p.h. and could climb 1 in 95 inclines

A large area of open land situated in Bordesley Green Road facing the main offices had previously been used as a brickworks, but was now derelict and this was acquired in 1904 for a massive expansion of the factory and as a vehicle test area.

The first building planned was a single storey Repair Shop 150 feet long by 32 feet, with a 3 feet 6 inches wide pit running almost

BELOW: A general view of the Machine Shop with enormous overhead lineshafts used to drive individual machines by a series of pulleys and belts. The machine in the centre foreground appears to be set up for machining gears which formed part of the gearbox. By 1914 the machine shop had expanded to take up the whole of the original 1901 building and had also encompassed the Foundry and Erecting Shop extensions built in 1902, with a total of 1,420 machine tools installed. By then it was divided into 8 sections, 1) Auto Turning Machines, 2) Gear Cutting, 3) Auto Screw Machines, 4) Miscellaneous Machines, 5) Hand Operated Capstans, 6) Milling Machines, 7) Drilling, and 8) Inspection Dept.

WOLSELEY TOOL & MOTOR CAR CO. LTD.
PROPOSED EAST WORKS SITE 1904 — 1906

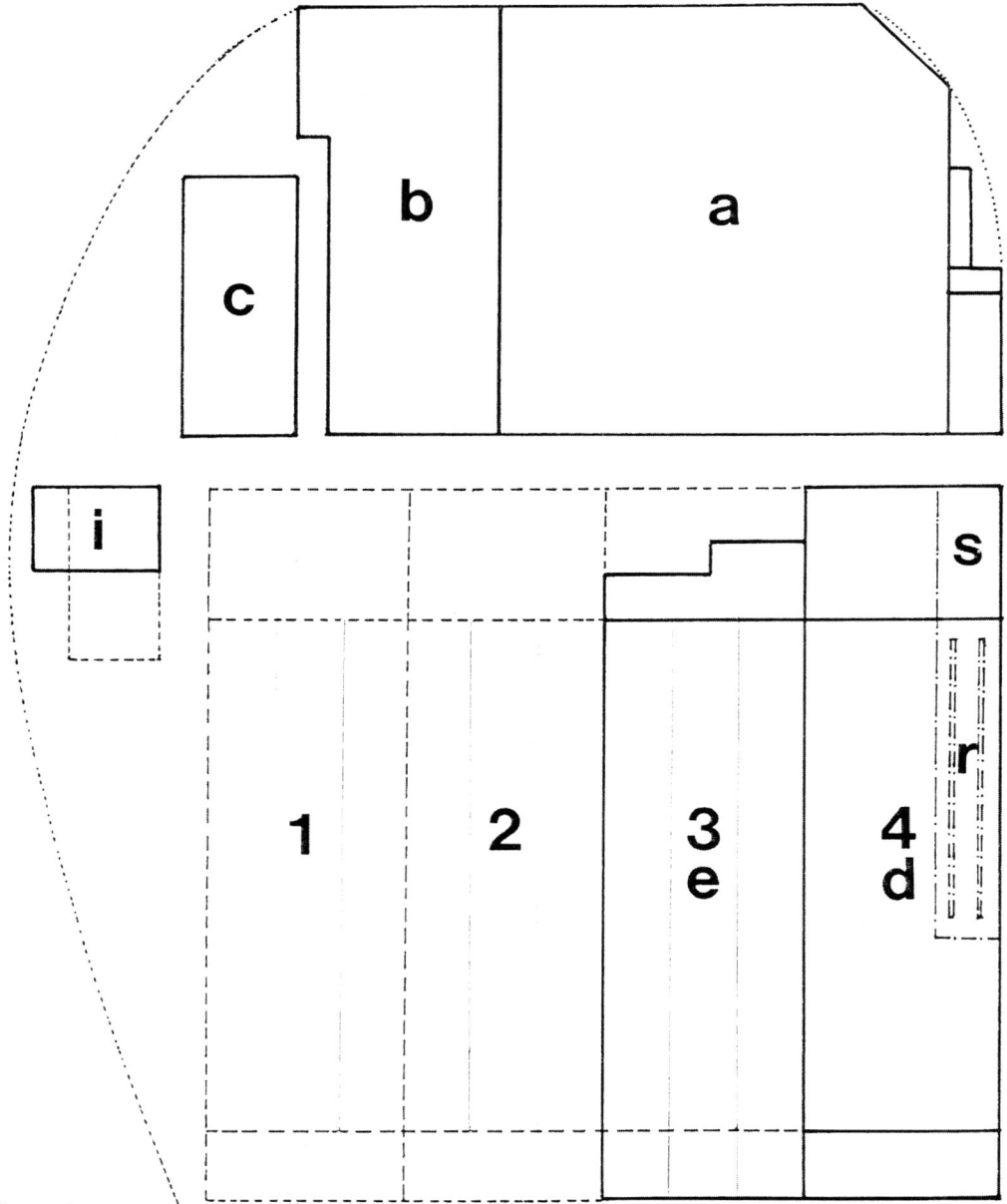

SCALE IN FEET

0   50   100   150   200

the complete length of the building, together with a two storey Stores to the rear of the repair shop 60 feet by 32 feet and containing a lift connecting the two floors. The height of the new building was to be 24 feet 2 inches to the eaves and 38 feet to the ridge, the building running in an east-west direction parallel to the railway embankment on the south side of the site.

By December the plans had been amended to provide a Mill consisting of two bays 29 feet 5 inches wide by 150 feet long, plus the Repair Shop which now had two pits running the length of the building. The Stores to the rear were to be extended across the full width of the Mill and Repair Shop and a two storey Warehouse was to be provided across the front of the Mill 30 feet long and a Washing Space, also 30 feet long provided at the front of the Repair Shop. The Repair Shop was to be devoted to the servicing and repair of customers cars, including cars damaged in accidents.

However, the largest building proposed in 1904 was for an Upholstering and Paint Shop, to be erected on the new Wolseley East Works site to the rear of the Mill and Repair Shop, 200 feet by 200 feet, built in ten 20 feet wide bays and measuring 16 feet high to the eaves and 25 feet 6 inches high to the ridges. Production at the Adderley Park works was now running at 9 cars per week and plans were being considered to start a night shift to cope with demand.

In 1904 Austin applied for eight patents, numbers 98, 5852, 6779, 7628, 9604, 19867, 21812 and 24533 covering engines, lever and quadrant gear changes, ball bearings, lubricators, propelling ships and a motor vehicle transmission. This latter patent, number 9604, is again of particular interest as it shows the design for a motor car powered by a four cylinder vertical engine with the gearbox bolted directly onto the engine, the drive then going through a short shaft to a chassis frame mounted transmission housing, then via chains to each rear wheel.

The patent dealing with propelling ships by various forms of drive gives an early indication of how diverse the company would become in succeeding years when it would be involved with marine engines, industrial engines and aircraft engines.

Indeed, in 1904 the company built a small railway shunting engine for a company in the north of England, the loco being of 2ft 9½ins gauge and powered by a two cylinder horizontal engine with a bore of 6 inches diameter and stroke of 7 inches which developed 20 b.h.p. at 600 r.p.m. With four 18 inch diameter wheels coupled together and driven by chains the loco had a gearbox giving two forward and two reverse speeds, was equipped with a 10 gallon fuel tank, weighed 3 tons and was capable of hauling 30 tons on a level track. Whilst building work continued on the East Works site a short stretch of railway track was laid and the loco tested at the factory before being shipped to the unknown customer, but was probably one of the Vickers factories.

In February 1904 the company introduced a new automatic carburetter and prospective customers were invited to try out cars with the new device in the grounds of Crystal Palace.

In November 1904 the company built a heavy duty tractor powered by a 24 h.p. two cylinder engine, but no further details appear to have been published and a 60 h.p. engine was also built to power a motor launch.

DIAGRAM

PROPOSED EAST WORKS SITE 1904 - 1906
This diagram illustrates the extent of the original proposals for the East Works site, in broken lines, and how it was actually built, in complete lines.

KEY

a. Upholstering & Paint Shop, 200 feet by 200 feet, built January 1905.
b. Body Shop, 200 feet by 75 feet built June 1906.
c. Coachsmiths Shop 120 feet by 50 feet, built June 1906. 4d. Full black lines show Mill Number 4 as built in 1905, including the original Repair Shop and Stores 'r' and 's'. Only Mill Number 4 had Offices built across the front of the building.
3e. Mill Number 3, full black lines show how it was built in 1905, 272 feet by 88 feet 6 inches, plus small Stores at rear.
i. Engine House, in broken lines as originally planned and in full lines as built in August 1905, 55 feet by 40 feet.
1-2. The broken lines show the position of Mill Numbers 1 & 2, as originally planned in January 1905 which, together with Mill Numbers 3 & 4 would have made this building 354 feet by 335 feet, which would have included the Offices at the front of the building and Stores to the rear.
r-s. In January 1904 the only buildings planned for the East Works site were the Repair Shop 'r', 150 feet by 32 feet.(containing two pits running almost the complete length of the building, as shown by the dash/dotted lines) and a Store 's' 60 feet by 32 feet.

Racing cars continued to be developed and a 96 h.p. model was built for the Gordon Bennett Trials in the Isle of Man, this particular car having a wheelbase of 9ft 0in, track of 4ft 7ins and was fitted with 36"x5" tyres on the back and 34"x3½" tyres on the front.

A fire appliance for Leicester Fire Brigade was also built using a special chassis powered by a 24 h.p. four cylinder engine and, with a four speed gearbox, had a top speed of about 25 m.p.h.

A "Colonial Car" was also built to carry six passengers, plus 10 cwts of mail or luggage, the passenger seats being fitted longitudinally to the rear of the vehicle. Powered by a 24 h.p. four cylinder engine and fitted with a four speed gearbox the vehicle weighed 30 cwts.

The building of 'one-off' vehicles by motor manufacturers was possible by reason of the very low production rates and, the desire by early manufacturers to provide whatever a potential customer required, unlike in later years when the process of mass production would almost certainly eliminate such vehicles from being made.

PHOTOGRAPHS

LEFT-TOP: During construction work on the East Works site a severe gale in January 1905 wreaked havoc to the roof of the new Upholstering & Paint Shop and this picture shows the extent of the damage. The three gable ends in the background formed Mill Number 4 of the proposed expansion on this site (Mill Number 3 had yet to be built alongside it) and in the distant background, to the right, can be seen the Main Office block and the chimney stack of the boiler house situated in West Works.

BOTTOM: There were quite a number of Coachsmiths Shops around the works, but this picture is thought to have been taken in building 'c' located in the East Works, and erected in 1906. The coachsmiths made metal fittings such as support brackets, levers and body fittings, using a variety of tools, some of which can be seen hanging on the wall next to the smithy's hearth.

ABOVE: Built in 1904 this narrow gauge industrial shunting locomotive was powered by a two cylinder 20 h.p. horizontal petrol engine, weighed 3 tons and could haul up to 30 tons. The driver sat sideways in the cab with his feet hanging over the side and could, presumably, sit on either side. Although the customer was never revealed it could have been the Vickers factory in Barrow in Furness.

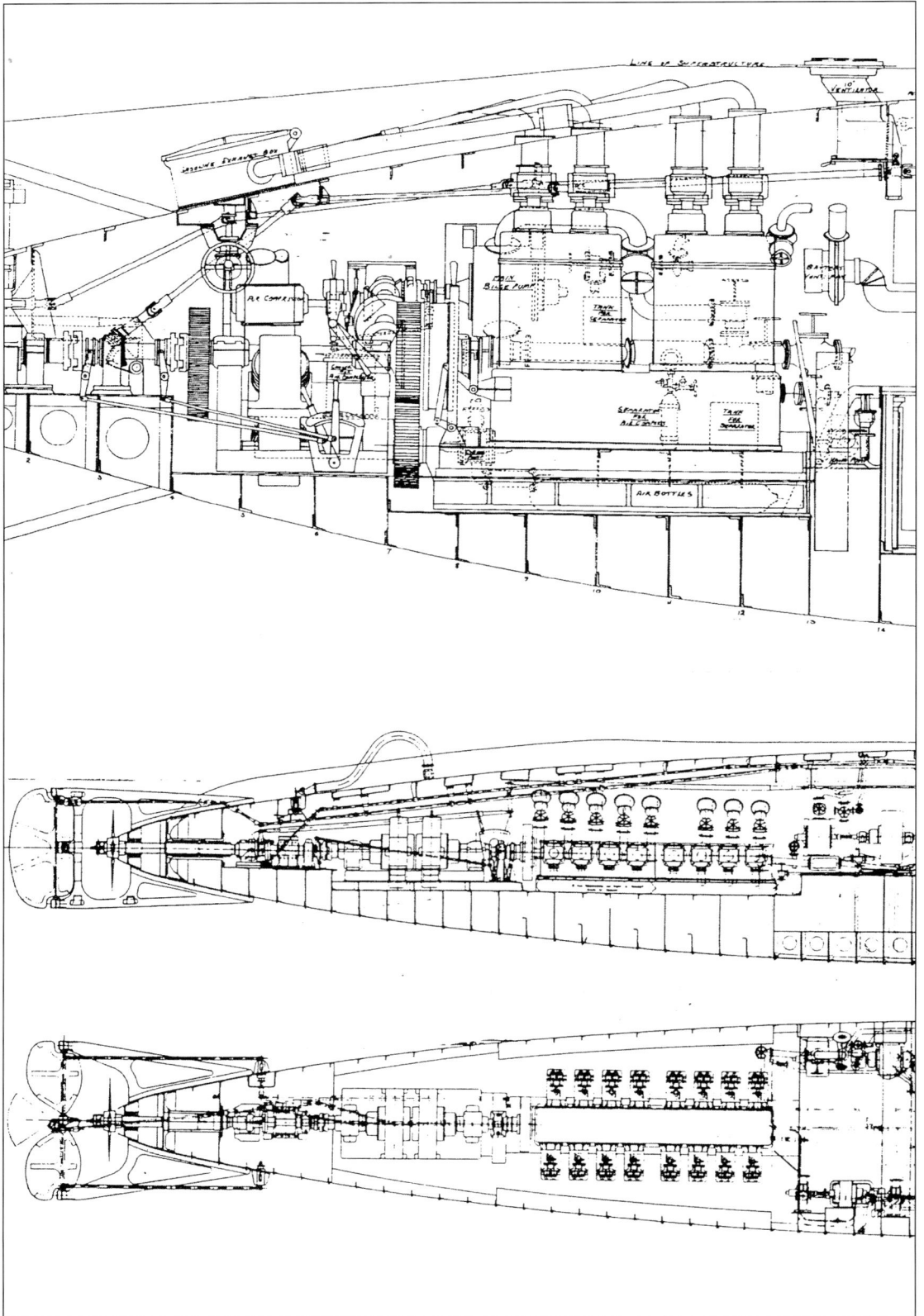

Various labels visible on the engineering drawing include: LINE OF SUPERSTRUCTURE, 10" VENTILATOR, GASOLINE EXHAUST BOX, AIR COMPRESSOR, MAIN BILGE PUMP, SEPARATOR FOR AIR & SAND, TANK FOR SEPARATOR, AIR BOTTLES

SUBMARINE ENGINES

The company had become involved with the design and construction of engines for submarines, apparently from about 1905. A total of three engines were built, of enormous proportions, all being 16 cylinder units of horizontal configuration with the cylinders cast in pairs and bolted to the crankcases which were probably made by bolting together two eight cylinder crankcases.

The first five British "Holland" Class submarines were fitted with four cylinder vertical petrol engines which, according to some nautical sources, were also designed by Wolseley. However, a recently discovered drawing casts some doubt on this idea as the engines appear to have been designed by the Otto Gas Engine Works in the U.S.A. One likely explanation could be that the drawing was supplied to Wolseley from America and the five engines were made at Adderley Park. These engines had a bore of 11.25" diameter and stroke of 14" and developing 160 b.h.p. at 320 r.p.m. With a specific fuel consumption of 0.875 lbs/bhp-hr the installed fuel consumption was about 20 gallons per hour. The engine had an overall length of 9' 1.75", width of 3' 2.5" and a height of 6' 7.5" with a total weight of 7.52 tons.

The 16 cylinder engines all differed in their bore and stroke dimensions and although all three had been rated at 600 h.p. by the company only the final engine achieved its designed output, showing a rapid learning curve by the Wolseley engine design team led by Alfred Remington. This was a tremendous achievement when one considers that the company had only been in existence for a few years and the internal combustion engine itself was a relatively new invention and yet the company was not only designing, but manufacturing these enormous engines.

Engine number one was fitted into the "A" Class submarine A1, had a bore of 8.5" diameter and stroke of 10" to give a capacity of 148 litres. This engine developed 350 b.h.p. at 400 r.p.m., was 14' 1.5" long, 6' 2.5" wide, 2' 1.5" high and weighed 17.1 tons. Engine number two, fitted into submarine A2-4, was the largest of all the submarine engines, with a bore and stroke of 12" giving a capacity of 355 litres and developing 450 b.h.p. at 400 r.p.m. Weighing 17.7 tons it was 19' 1.5" long, 8' 1" wide and 4' 6" high and returned an installed fuel consumption of about 70 gallons per hour. The third engine was fitted into submarine A5-12 and had a bore of 11.25" diameter, stroke of 12", a capacity of 312 litres and developed 600 b.h.p. at 400 r.p.m. The dimensions of this engine were, 18' 10" long, 7' 9.375" wide, 3' 8.5" high and weighed 16.2 tons. With the successful development of the 16 cylinder engine to produce its designed output the further development and manufacture of this engine was taken over by the parent company Vickers of Barrow in Furness who made five more engines with the same bore and stroke dimensions as engine number three, their final engine producing 668 b.h.p. at 400 r.p.m. and returning a specific fuel consumption of 0.664 lbs/bhp-hr compared with 0.895 lbs/bhp-hr for the Wolseley built engine number three. After building their fifth 16 cylinder engine Vickers changed the design to a 12 cylinder unit with the same bore and stroke dimensions and still developing 600 b.h.p., but which reduced the overall length by 4 feet and saved one ton in weight.

ILLUSTRATION

TOP: This detail is taken from an engineering drawing of a British "Holland" Class submarine. These were the first of a whole generation of submarines built in this country and which defended our shores in both the First and Second World Wars.

This drawing shows the installation of one of the 4 cylinder vertical petrol engines which is now the subject of some speculation as regards its assignment to Wolseley.

The engine crankshaft was lower than the main propeller shaft which was driven through the reduction gearing shown at the front of the engine which gave a ratio of 1.9:1. The engine was also used to drive a dynamotor for charging batteries and for submerged sailing, an air compressor for charging the high pressure air bottles and a large bilge pump.

The individual exhaust pipes can be seen above the engine, the pipes bending sharply to the stern of the vessel into a large exhaust box. Six hundred gallons of petrol were stored in one tank in the bow of the vessel beneath the torpedo tube and with petrol being used at about 20 gallons per hour the engine could only be run for a maximum of 30 hours.

An explosion occurred in "Holland" No.2 caused by petrol vapour being ignited when an electric switch was operated and several members of the crew were badly burned. Ultimately, this led to the abandonment of petrol engines in favour of diesels which used a less flammable fuel.

BOTTOM: A small section from a drawing of the British 'A' Class submarine, 'A1', showing the installation of the Wolseley 16 cylinder, 148 litre, horizontal petrol engine which had exhaust valves 5" in diameter, was over 14ft long and weighed 17 tons. The engines were cooled by sea water circulated by an engine driven pump, but with little chance to attain a normal running temperature the engines were obviously not running efficiently, as is shown by their installed specific fuel consumption of 0.8 lbs/ bhp hour.

THE 6-H.P. SIDDELEY LIGHT CAR.

Fig. 1. Side view of the 6-h.p. Siddeley Chassis, showing the simple arrangement of the well-protected Driving Mechanism.

PRICE:—With 2 seated body, £190; with 3 seated £200.

Cape Cart Hood, suitable for 3 seated body, £15   Glass Wind Screen, £6 10 0

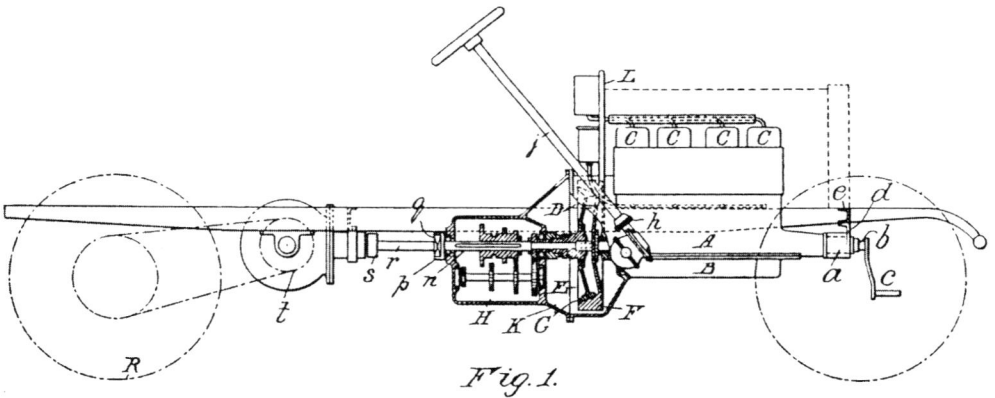

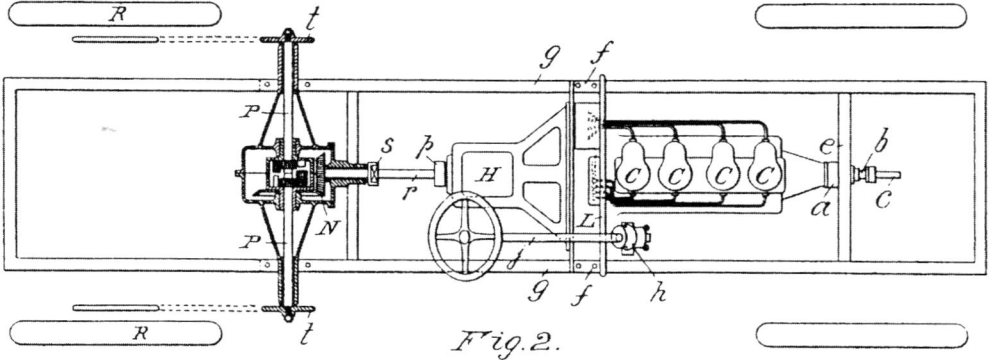

Fig. 1.

Fig. 2.

In January of 1905, Vickers Sons & Maxim Ltd., announced that a 12 h.p. car was to be built for Siddeley at the Crayford Works where the Wolseley 'Voiturette' was already being built and which employed 2,100 men. The Siddeley car was to be powered by a two cylinder vertical engine with a bore and stroke of $4\frac{1}{2}$", developing 12 h.p. at 850 r.p.m. and fitted with a 4 speed gearbox. The cars were built at the Crayford Works as 'running chassis', then transported by rail to Adderley Park to have bodies fitted and for painting.

One of the first examples of the new 12 h.p. Siddeley cars was sent on a 5,000 mile observed trial which it completed in mid February, using 307 gallons of petrol, at a cost of £15-7s-0d, plus 8.25 gallons of oil at a cost of £1-4s-9d.

Siddeley had been building 6 h.p. and 8 h.p. cars previously and in February Mr. J. D. Siddeley announced that he had sold his motor car business to Wolseley and had been appointed their Sales Manager. Even Mrs Siddeley was in the news after taking driving instruction from her husband and observed driving a Wolseley car in London accompanied by a mechanic.

A show at Olympia in February enabled the company to demonstrate just how diversified their product range had become where they had four stands to exhibit motor cars, heavy vehicles, motor boats and machine tools.

A 3 ton lorry had recently been supplied to the Great Western Railway company which had a wheelbase of 10ft 6ins, track of 6ft 2ins, overall width of 7ft 2ins, overall length of 18ft and an unladen weight of 50 cwts. The lorry had a canvas tilt covering the load platform, which was 11ft 6ins long and had a loading height of 2ft 7ins. Fitted with a two cylinder horizontal engine having a bore of $6\frac{1}{2}$" diameter and stroke of $7\frac{1}{2}$" developing 20 h.p. at 600 r.p.m., the lorry had a 12 gallon petrol tank fitted giving it a range of about 80 miles, returning a little under 7 m.p.g. In March a new racing car was announced fitted with a more powerful four cylinder horizontal engine developing 90 h.p. at 1,000 r.p.m., the car having a wheelbase of 8ft 8ins and track of 4ft 7ins.

In June Herbert Austin was appointed Chairman of the British Empire Motor Trades Alliance, but in the same month Austin, at the age of 39, resigned from the Wolseley company, apparently, because he was determined to retain horizontal engines in Wolseley cars despite overwhelming evidence that these had been abandoned by other motor car companies in favour of vertical engines. Austin had placed his opinions on record in a Wolseley catalogue, as follows:-

"The vertical type of engine always was and always will be, far more difficult to lubricate satisfactorily than the horizontal type. Some makers of vertical engines try to throw discredit on the horizontal type by saying that the weight of the piston wears the liner oval. This is all nonsense, because the angular thrust of the connecting rod in both types causes a far greater pressure to be put on one side of the liner than a dozen pistons would weigh, and yet with proper lubrication no wear takes place....the normal speed of our motor is 750 r.p.m. and this is quite fast enough to allow of any long usage. Motors which run at 1,000 to 2,000 r.p.m. have, of necessity, only a short life."

ILLUSTRATION

This 1905 6 h.p. Light Car was designed by Wolseley for the Siddeley Autocar Company and was built at the Crayford Works. The vertical single cylinder engine had a bore of $4\frac{1}{2}$" diameter and stroke of $4\frac{1}{2}$", giving it a capacity of 1.173 litres, with a working speed range of 850 r.p.m. to 1,800 r.p.m. The 3 speed and reverse gearbox was unit mounted with the engine and an open propshaft drove the bevel gear rear axle. It is believed that only a small number of these cars were built, numbering no more than about 50 chassis.

DIAGRAM

PATENT NUMBER 9604
Dated 27th April, 1904, this patent covers the design for mounting a vertical engine in a motor car chassis. Like patent number 22225, the engine uses three mounting points, one to the front and two to the rear of the engine, but in this design the clutch and gearbox are bolted directly to the flywheel end of the engine casing and the rear engine mountings are also designed to carry other mechanical units such as the clutch and brake controls, the steering box and the dashboard assembly. This allows the removal of all these components in one operation. The gearbox in this design is connected to a transverse differential/drive unit mounted across the chassis frame, via a short drive shaft, the drive then being carried to each side of the vehicle and transmitted to each rear wheel by chain drives.

This patent was applied for by Herbert Austin and quite clearly show that, despite his alleged dislike of the vertical engine, designs for motor cars fitted with such engines were already coming from his drawing board in 1903 and 1904. Could all the rhetoric have been to disinform his opponents whilst he quietly worked away on such designs? Perhaps we will never know!

(BMIHT photo) A 10 cwt Royal Mail van is seen here driving through one of the two gateways to the Adderley Park East Works. The picture gives an excellent view of the main office building rected in 1897 (the date can be seen in the stonework of the building immediately above the van) and shows it with the original windows to the ground floor which had been used as stores and warehousing. By 1914 these windows had been changed to the sash type windows of the upper floor. The company name across the front of the building was cast in solid bronze and in later years was hidden from view by the name Morris Commercial Cars Ltd., who moved into the works in 1929. The brick and stone pillars supporting the very ornate railings were to survive into the 1960's, somehow managing to escape the austerity measures of the Second World War when steel railings were removed from even the most prestigious buildings in Britain to fuel the war machine.

Austin appears not to have considered the relationship of piston speed with cylinder wear and the localised cooling problems associated with horizontal engines even today. However, had Austin become so resolute, to the point of being obdurate about the horizontal engine, why was he already patenting designs for vertical engined cars in 1903-1904, and why upon leaving Wolseley and starting the Austin Motor Company Limited did he produce, not horizontal engined cars, but 25/30 h.p. four cylinder vertical engined cars? For a man who resigned from a responsible position in a rapidly expanding and already reputable company, allegedly on a matter of principle, it is difficult to understand why this principle was abandoned, apparently as soon as he walked away from the company.

Possibly another reason for Austin's resignation was that the parent company, Vickers, were putting him in an increasingly impossible position, having opened up the Crayford Works to produce the 'Vioturette', which Austin could not possibly supervise personally, and then purchasing the Siddeley car business which had once been a competitor to Wolseley, and employing the overtly ambitious Siddeley himself in a position from which he could start to dictate Wolseley's future product range.

Following Austin's departure Mr J.D.Siddeley, of the Siddeley Autocar Company, was appointed General Manager of the Wolseley Tool & Motor Car Company Ltd., and Alfred A. Remington, who had become Chief Draughtsman in 1902, became responsible for dealing with patents and became Designer in 1907, with another talented draughtsman, Arthur Rowledge as Chief Draughtsman. (Remington had been an apprentice with Kynoch Limited in Birmingham and took up an appointment as a draughtsman with the Wolseley Sheep Shearing Machine Company Limited in 1900 and transferred to the Wolseley Tool & Motor Car Company Limited in 1901. Born in Sutton Coldfield near Birmingham in 1877 Remington was forced to leave Wolseley in 1920, due to ill health, and died in 1922. Obviously a very talented engineer in his own right one suspects that his input into the fledgling Wolseley motor company was on a par to that of Austin himself.)

Meanwhile, expansion of the factory continued with plans for the East Works site being amended to increase the size of the Mill and Repair Shop to a building comprising twelve bays each 29 feet 5 inches wide with Stores to the rear running the full width of the building and Offices and Warehouses the full width of the front of the building, the overall dimensions of this building being 360 feet by 334 feet. An Engine House was also proposed for the East Works site measuring 92 feet by 38 feet to provide electric power and the Upholstering & Paint Shop was to be provided with toilets and a boiler house. (Construction of the Upholstering & Paint Shop had been hampered in January when a severe gale blew down parts of the new building adjacent to the railway embankment.)

However, the plans were amended again with the Engine House being reduced to 55 feet by 40 feet and containing two large gas engines, but interestingly, the walls of this building were 18" thick to contain the effects of any explosions which might take place. The proposed enlarged Mill and Repair Shop was also reduced in size and in reality ended up as a building measuring only 180 feet by 334 feet.

About this time a car test track had been built around the perimeter of the East Works site and a special 1 in 3½ incline built to test the hill climbing abilities of the cars. Cars would be tested as loaded chassis around the test track, put through the Repair Shop (Rectification Shop as we would call it today) to have any repairs or adjustments made and then passed to the Body Shop to have the correct type of body fitted ordered by the customer. The test track was also used to evaluate experimental cars in the process of being developed.

Remington lost no time after the departure of Austin and applied for thirteen patents in 1905, numbers 667, 2648, 4054, 6019, 6800, 14094, 14643, 15756, 16436, 19279, 19320, 20342 and 25917. The subjects covered included, valve gear for internal combustion engines, radiators, pressurised fuel supply for engines, change speed mechanism, brake gear and ball bearings.(The company made most of its own ball bearings, with the exception of the steel balls, which it bought in from a specialist supplier). Some of the engine patents deal particularly with larger industrial engines showing that the diversification policy of the company was continuing even after Austin's departure. Patent number 15756 dealing with the improved construction of radiators is also of significant interest as it was taken out jointly by Robert Raymond Brown, Secretary of Wolseley and Louis Silverman of the Crayford Works in Kent.

The 1905 range of cars consisted of a 6 h.p. single cylinder model, 8 h.p. and 12 h.p. twin cylinder models, all with horizontal engines, and a sign of the times, a "Wolseley - Siddeley" 15 h.p. car with a four cylinder vertical engine having a bore and stroke of 4". In September two cars were prepared for the forthcoming Tourist

PHOTOGRAPH

A Cabriolet body being built in building 'b' of the East Works. The bodies were made individually by skilled carpenters using very simple jigs, like the two seen here holding up the vertical door posts, leaving the carpenter with both hands free to continue his work. These were skilled men who had probably learned their trade in the carriage and coach building companies in and around Birmingham.

In 1914 over 200 body builders were employed by the company, making 40 bodies per week, and the timber stores held a stock of seasoned timber for body building worth £10,000.

Trophy Race, both being powered by 18 h.p. four cylinder Siddeley engines with a bore and stroke of 102mm and having four speed gearboxes, a wheelbase of 8ft 6ins and track of 4ft 0ins. In the same month a special Shooting Brake was delivered to The Mackintosh of Mackintosh, based on a 18 h.p. chassis and a 15 h.p. Siddeley car was awarded a Gold Medal in the Town Motor Carriage Competition.

For the 1906 season cars became a mixture of "Wolseley" and "Siddeley" models, settling down to just "Siddeley" models for the 1907 season, and then "Wolseley-Siddeley" later, until two years after the departure of J.D.Siddeley in 1909 when the Wolseley name was again used exclusively across the whole range.

A more detailed look at the 1906 cars reveals that the single cylinder 6 h.p. light car chassis was powered by a horizontal engine with a bore of 4.5" diameter, stroke of 5", giving a capacity of 1.3 litres, a maximum speed of 800 r.p.m. and was fitted with a half compression cam for starting. Based on a pressed steel chassis frame with a wheelbase of 5ft 6ins, and with a track of 4ft, the transmission consisted of a "silent" chain from the engine to the 3 speed gearbox mounted clutch, then via a single roller chain to the live rear axle with differential gear. Braking was via a pedal operated band brake on the rear axle, with hand lever operated band brakes at the rear wheels. This chassis cost £160, ex.works.

The 8 h.p. and 12 h.p. "Wolseley" chassis were of very similar construction, but whereas the 8 h.p. model had a wheelbase of 7ft 2ins, the 12 h.p. model had a wheelbase of 8ft 6ins and had an extra 2.5ins on the track, at 4ft 3ins. Both models were powered by twin cylinder horizontal engines, the 8 h.p. engine having a bore of 4" diameter, stroke of 4", with a capacity of 1.6 litres, and the 12 h.p. engine having a bore of 4.5" diameter, stroke of 5", capacity of 2.6 litres, with the smaller engine being the faster of the two, by 50 r.p.m., with a speed of 900 r.p.m. Transmission on both models was via an engine mounted clutch, via "silent" chain to the 4 speed gearbox/transverse differential housing, then via roller chains to both rear wheels. The 8 hp. model had a top road speed of about 26 m.p.h. and the 12 h.p. model was faster at 33 m.p.h. The same braking system was used for both models, with pedal operated double acting internal brakes inside drums fitted to the rear road wheels, and lever operated band brakes on drums which were part of the rear wheel drive sprockets. The prices of these two models, in chassis form, was £255 and £325 respectively.

A "Siddeley" 12 h.p. model was also listed, and although fitted with a slightly smaller 2.3 litre 2 cylinder engine, it was of vertical build and had a bore and stroke of 4.5". A leather faced cone clutch was fitted to the engine which then transmitted power via a short open propshaft to the 3 speed gearbox, then via open propshaft to the 'live' bevel gear rear axle. Braking was via a pedal operated, metal to metal, hinged block type brake fitted to the rear of the gearbox, and via lever operated internal drum brakes at the rear road wheels. With a track of 4ft 3.5ins and wheelbase of 9ft 6ins this chassis cost £325.

A 15 h.p. "Siddeley" model based upon an almost identical chassis frame to the 12 h.p. model, featured a 4 cylinder vertical engine with a bore and stroke of 4", giving a capacity of 3.3 litres, but with a maximum speed of 1,000 r.p.m. The transmission and braking systems were virtually identical to the smaller 12 h.p.

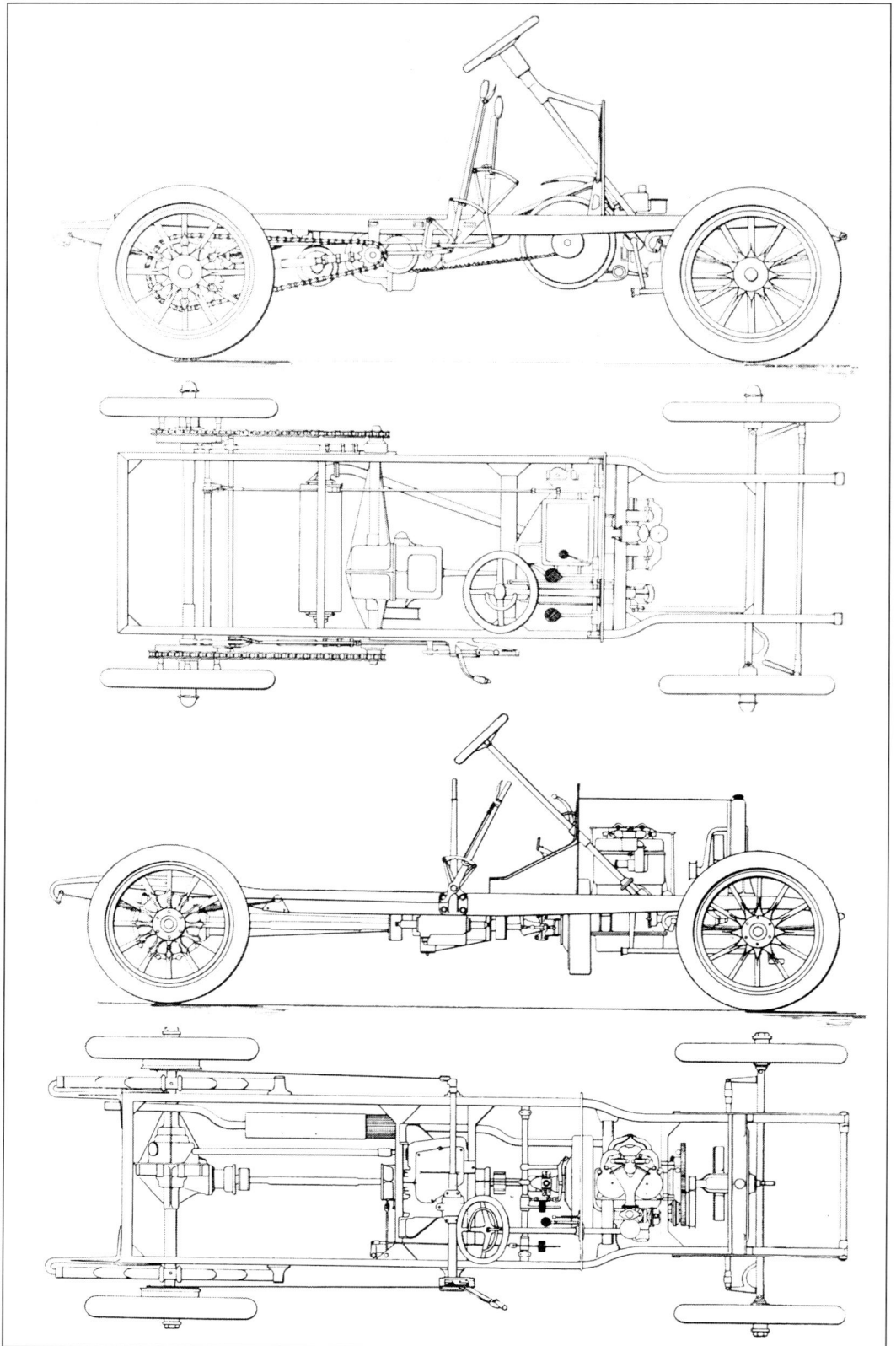

Two interesting drawings of 12 h.p. chassis available in the 1906 transition period when vertical engines were replacing horizontal engines in most of Wolseley's range of motor cars.

The top illustration shows the 12 h.p. Wolseley with its twin cylinder horizontal engine mounted transversely across the chassis frame with the cylinders facing forwards. The drive from the flywheel end of the engine, which was just beneath the drivers feet, was via a Renold's silent chain to the transverse 4 speed gearbox cum differential housing. Drive to each rear wheel was also by chains, the rear axle itself being a solid steel bar with the wheels mounted on plain phosphor bronze bearings.

The front axle was a forged beam with the steering track rod mounted forward of the axle, the steering itself being of the worm and sector type.

The exhaust system included a transversely mounted silencer fitted to the rear of the gearbox/differential housing, clearly shown in the plan view of the motor car chassis.

The lower drawing shows the "Siddeley" 12 h.p. chassis fitted with a 2 cylinder vertical engine mounted in the chassis frame forward of the dashboard, and shown here complete with cooling fan and radiator.

The exhaust system on this model was led along the nearside of the chassis to a silencer fitted longitudinally between the gearbox rear crossmember and the rear axle.

The clutch was engine mounted and connected to the remotely mounted 3 speed gearbox by a short open propshaft, and then by a second propshaft to the live bevel gear drive rear axle. Gearchanging was executed via a remote gear change lever mounted to the right hand side of the drivers seat, the quadrant also forming the pivot for the hand lever operated internal drum type brakes.

On this model the front axle steering track rod was fitted to the rear of the forged axle bed.

Two quite different designs to provide a 12 h.p. motor car and it is notable that the horizontal engined model required the chassis frame to be mounted quite high to provide adequate ground clearance for the engine which was, substantially, below the floor, which also meant more difficult access for the driver and passengers. Furthermore, the weight distribution on the horizontal engined model appears to be inferior to the more conventional vertical engined car, the former probably having a very lightly laden front axle.

model and the chassis cost £425.

The remaining four "Siddeley" models, comprising a 18 h.p., 25 h.p., 32 h.p. and 70 h.p. 4 cylinder vertical engined chassis were all of similar mechanical construction with engine mounted leather faced cone clutch driving into a combined gearbox/transverse differential housing via a short open propshaft, and then by roller chains to each rear wheel. On all models, except the 70 h.p. chassis, had 4 speed gearboxes, but the largest model could only be had with a 3 speed gearbox.

Engine data was as follows:- 18 h.p., bore of 4.25" diameter and stroke of 4", capacity 3.7 litres, with a normal speed of 1,000 r.p.m.; 25 h.p., bore of 4.5" diameter, stroke of 5", capacity of 5.2 litres, and speed of 900 r.p.m.; 32 h.p., bore of 5.25" diameter, stroke of 5", capacity of 7 litres, and speed of 900 r.p.m., and the mighty 70 h.p. with a bore of 6.5" diameter, stroke of 5", giving a massive capacity of 13 litres, and with a speed of 1,000 r.p.m., all these being vertical engines.

The braking system of the 18 h.p. chassis comprised pedal operated metal to metal brakes inside drums attached to the rear road wheel sprockets, and lever operated band brakes on the drums attached to the rear road wheel sprockets. The 25 h.p. and 32 h.p. chassis had pedal operated internal metal to metal brakes inside drums attached to the sprockets on the rear road wheels, and lever/cable operated band brakes working on the drums attached to the rear wheel sprockets. On the 70 h.p. model three different brakes were provided, comprising a double acting block brake working on a drum fitted to the front end of the gearbox and operated by a pedal inter-connected with the clutch pedal, pedal operated internal metal to metal brakes inside drums attached to the rear wheel sprockets, and lever operated band brakes on the rear wheel drums.

Suspension on all models throughout the range was by conventionally mounted semi-elliptic steel leaf springs, with the front springs mounted directly beneath the chassis frame side members on all models; rear springs mounted beneath the chassis frame on 8 h.p., 12 h.p. and 18 h.p. chassis, and with the remainder of the models having their rear springs mounted to the outside of the chassis frame sidemembers. As yet, there was no indication of Wolseley's experiments with the design of the rear suspension of their motor cars to improve ride and handling qualities, but this patented design would eventually be fitted across almost the whole range of motor car chassis.

The 18 h.p. chassis was available with a choice of 9ft 6ins, or 10ft 6ins wheelbase at £525 and £550 respectively, the 25 h.p. and 32 h.p. chassis were available with 10ft or 11ft 6ins wheelbases and cost £625 or £650 25 h.p., and £750 and £775 for the 32 h.p. chassis. The 70 h.p. chassis had a wheelbase of 10ft 11ins and front track of 4ft 7ins, and cost £1250.

The standard range of factory built bodies included a 2 seat Bucket Phaeton suitable for the 6 h.p. chassis only at £15, a 4 seat Tonneau for the 8 h.p. chassis at £45, a 4 seat Special Side Entrance Phaeton suitable for the 18 h.p., 25 h.p. and 32 h.p. chassis at £125, a 12 seater Shooting Brake with two longitudinal seats to the rear for the 25 h.p. or 32 h.p. chassis at £125, and a 6 seat Double Landaulette, with the luxury of a canopy and screen for the drivers compartment, and suitable for the 18 h.p., 25 h.p. and 32 h.p. chassis at £210. As well as these standard bodies customers could,

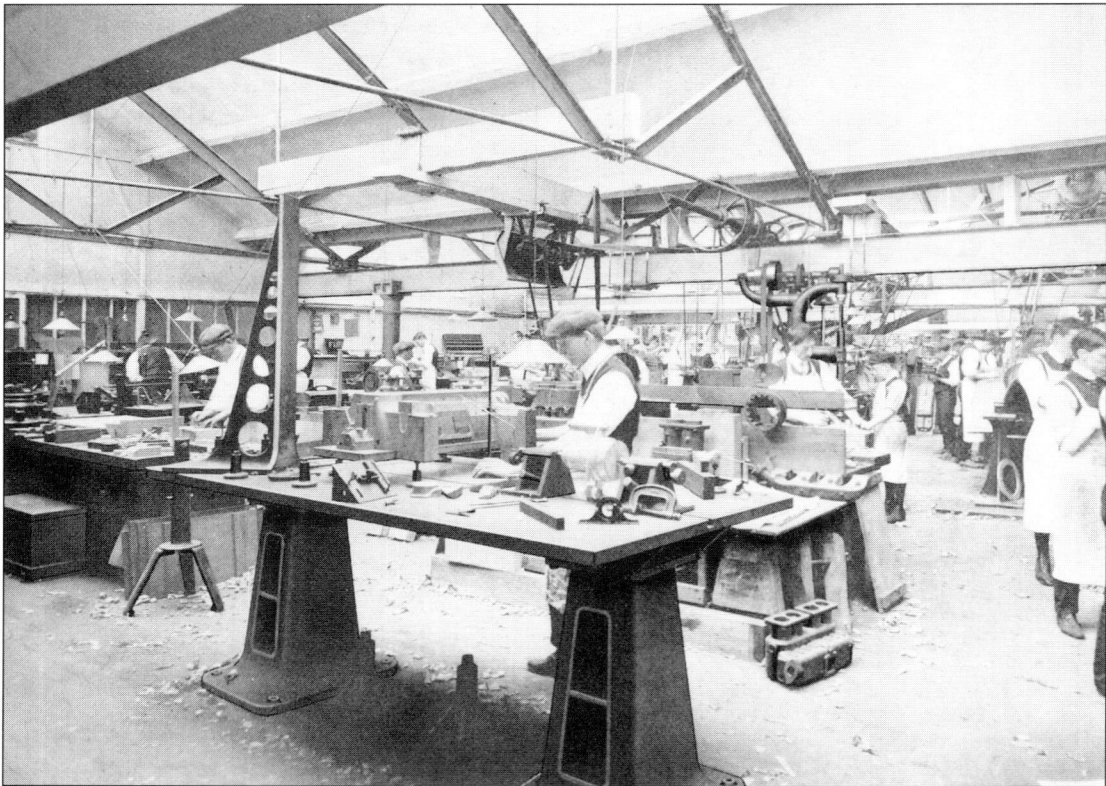

of course, order any body style they wished, as long as it was compatible with the chassis, and at a cost reflecting the highly specialised workmanship put into its construction.

The East Works was expanded again in 1906 by the erection of a building measuring 75 feet by 200 feet, adjoining the Upholstering & Paint Shop, which housed a Body Shop 75 feet by 140 feet (with a Supervisors Office measuring 12 feet by 9 feet), a Wheeling Shop 39 feet by 75 feet and a Stores complete with timber drying kiln, 20 feet by 75 feet. Fifteen feet away from the body shop a second building was erected 50 feet by 120 feet to house a Coachsmiths Shop.

In July 1906 workers from the Adderley Park works set off for their annual works outing to Blackpool whilst their fellow workers from Crayford enjoyed a day out in Hastings.

Remington meanwhile appears to have had a relatively quiet year with only six patents being applied for by the company, numbers 734, 737, 2099, 5297, 8708 and 23171. Patent number 737 proposed a compressed air starting device for engines and number 23171 a device for cutting off the fuel supply automatically when a car descends a hill or the car is stopped and the engine switched off.

The British motor industry was expanding rapidly with new car makers appearing month by month, but just like today, we were importing more motor cars than we exported. The figures for the years, ending 1st January, 1904, 1905 and 1906 show that we imported cars totalling 335, 362 and 458 respectively and exported cars totalling 55, 77 and 146 respectively for those three years.

The commercial vehicle range in 1906 consisted of 2 cwt, 10 cwt and 20 cwt vans, powered by a single cylinder 6 h.p. engine, two cylinder 8 h.p. engine and two cylinder 12 h.p. engine respectively and 20 cwt, 60 cwt and 80 cwt lorries powered by two cylinder 20 h.p. engines and a four cylinder 24 h.p. engine, plus two omnibus chassis. The 2 cwt van was just a two seater motor car with a box behind the seats about the same height as the seat backrests and with a small vertically hinged door to the 'load compartment'.

PHOTOGRAPHS

TOP: Taken about 1910, this photograph shows the Pattern Making Shop where skilled craftsmen made the wooden patterns used in the process of casting components for motor cars. The very low roof and its form of construction would suggest that the Paint Shop and Trimming Shop (buildings 'm' and 'n') built in 1903 at the north end of the West Works main office block, had by this time been converted into the Pattern Shop and, a few years later, would be converted to a Drawing Office, a function it would retain into the later occupancy by Morris Commercial Cars Ltd.

BOTTOM: A general view of the Chassis Painting Department in 1910, situated in building 'a' in the East Works. The assembled chassis were hand painted before being passed on to the Body Mounting Shop nearby where the body required by the customer would be fitted, and final finishing undertaken before going into the Despatch Department.

The rear suspension fitted to some of these chassis should be noted, as it comprised a 3 spring design which was quite popular in the 19th century as the rear suspension of horse drawn carts and carriages. The inverted, semi-elliptic, steel leaf spring is mounted transversely and bolted at its centre to the chassis frame, or as in this instance, an extension to the chassis frame. The two longitudinal axle mounted springs are then connected to this spring by shackles.

WOLSELEY SIDDELEY · AUTOCARS · HOLD WORLD'S RECORD FOR RELIABILITY

The omnibus chassis being offered for the 1906 season comprised 22 and 36 passenger models powered by two cylinder 20 h.p. horizontal engines, or powered by four cylinder 24 h.p. horizontal engines, all models having four speed gearboxes. However, in April 1906 a new omnibus chassis was introduced powered by a four cylinder 30 h.p. vertical Siddeley engine having a bore of 4½" diameter and stroke of 5" and developed 33 h.p at 1,050 r.p.m. This semi-forward control model had a wheelbase of 12ft 0ins, track of 6ft 2ins and with an overall chassis length of 16ft 0ins. The London & General Omnibus Company had operated a number of Wolseley buses on a trial basis, but withdrew all the models fitted with horizontal engines and returned them to the factory as they had not proved to be very satisfactory. However, one of the new 30 h.p. models was performing well on the Cricklewood to Elephant & Castle route and covered 10,000 miles with only £5-0s-0d having been spent on repairs which encouraged the L.G.O.C., to place orders for a further 24 chassis, with another 50 chassis ordered for 1907-1908. Production of the new 30 h.p. model was currently running at 6 chassis per week and the company had orders for the whole 1906 production run. By September 1907 fourteen of the new L.G.O.C. buses had covered a total distance of 30,000 miles without any trouble or loss of time during running.

One Wolseley omnibus, a 22 seater powered by a 2 cylinder 20 h.p. horozontal engine, was put into service in Birmingham with the Birmingham Motor Express Company Limited on their City to Hagley Road service. This carried the registration number O 1281, but was withdrawn from service within a short time because it was found to be unreliable.

An unusual Fire Appliance was also built in 1906, based upon a semi-forward control bus chassis powered by a 24 h.p. horizontal engine, it had another engine mounted vertically behind the front seats to power pumps designed by a Mr. J.T. Scarborough. The engine driving the pumps was a four cylinder Wolseley marine engine with a bore of 6" diameter and stroke of 7" developing 60 h.p. at 600 r.p.m. A 'First Aid' Fire Appliance, powered by a 30 h.p. engine, capable of carrying 16 men at speeds up to 20 m.p.h. was supplied to the Birmingham Fire Brigade in March 1907.

Two 5 ton tractors and a 4 ton lorry were undergoing trials at the military establishment in Aldershot, the tractors being powered by four cylinder horizontal engines developing 30 h.p. at 800 r.p.m. and running on paraffin.

In 1907 and 1908 no building work took place at the factory and the range of cars available now included 10 h.p., 14 h.p., 18 h.p., 30 h.p., 40 h.p. and 45 h.p. models, all but the two last models employing bevel final drive. The 10 h.p. model had a twin cylinder engine, the rest being 4 cylinder engines except the 45 h.p. model which employed a 6 cylinder engine with a bore of 4.625" and stroke of 5". The 10 h.p. model was based on a 7ft 6ins wheelbase chassis and cost £300 complete with body; the 14 h.p. was based on a 8ft 9ins wheelbase chassis and cost £380 complete; the 18 h.p. model was based on a 9ft 9ins wheelbase chassis and cost £575; the 30 h.p. model was based on a 9ft 6ins wheelbase chassis and cost £625 and the 45 h.p. model had a wheelbase of 11ft 3ins and cost £975 complete with bodywork.

PHOTOGRAPHS

TOP: (BMIHT photo) Photographed in Bordesley Green Road across one of the entrances to the rapidly expanding East Works in 1906, is one of the 22 seater omnibuses supplied to the Birmingham Motor Express Company Limited for use on their Hagley Road service. The bus was powered by a 2 cylinder 20 h.p. horizontal engine, carried the registration number O 1281 (it is on Trade Plates here), but did not prove reliable and was withdrawn from service within a short time. The 'passengers' shown here were probably local people acquired by the photographer solely for this picture. The large wooden building in the background was a temporary structure used as a Car Test Shed, which actually survived until 1914 when it was removed to make way for extensions to the Shell Shop.

BOTTOM: The 1907 Wolseley-BTH petrol electric omnibus was used as a demonstrator, but did not succeed in getting any orders for this novel new form of passenger transport. One of the two electric traction motors, together with the chain drive to the rear wheels, can clearly be seen in this picture. (Photograph Courtesy of Birmingham Library Services)

LEFT-TOP: One of the two 200 h.p. eight cylinder marine engines built in 1908 to power a racing motor launch named "Wolseley -Siddeley". The engine is shown here mounted on an inclined test bed, to simulate its actual installation in the craft, and is coupled to a Heenan & Froude water dynamometer in one of the Adderley Park test houses. In the background a set of belt driven pulleys can be seen mounted on the wall which were sometimes used to drive an engine for a short time to 'run-in' the engine before it was started up under its own power for full performance testing. (Photograph Courtesy of Birmingham Library Services.)

BOTTOM: The racing motor launch "Wolseley-Siddeley" was later renamed "Ursula" and in this picture the launch can be seen at Monaco whilst breaking one of several records which the boat was ultimately to hold. Such was the durability of Wolseley marine engines, the boat was reputed to be capable of even higher speeds after 4 years of almost continual racing. "Ursula" was 49 feet long with a 6ft 6ins beam and had a displacement of 5.25 tons, and made from Honduras mahogany.

BELOW: "Angela ", a boat built in the East Cowes yard of the Wolseley Tool & Motor Car Co.Ltd., powered by a Wolseley marine engine, and seen here at full speed. During 1913 it had won eleven First Prizes during competitions at home and abroad, and was a British Motor Boat Club 21ft Class Racer.

Only three patents were applied for in 1907, numbers 9194, 9382 and 10268. Number 9382 describes a rotary type hydraulic shock absorber, interestingly the patent being taken out jointly by the Company and Andre Christophe and Paul Menteyne, described as Engineers, of Neuilly sur Seine, France (the company bought this patent and used this type of shock absorber on the 1907 cars). Patent number 10268 describes a motor car gearbox designed " with a view to quietness of running and compactness of space".

In March 1907 the company was running a demonstration petrol-electric bus from the Olympia Motor Show, this new model being developed jointly with the British Thomson Houston company of Rugby and powered by a 25 h.p. Wolseley engine, governed to 400 r.p.m. driving a large D.C. dynamo, the drive to the rear wheels being via two traction motors. This bus was later road tested from Rugby to Malvern and covered the 66.4 miles at an average speed of 15 m.p.h. and a petrol consumption of 7 m.p.g. A petrol electric platform lorry was also built and entered in the Industrial Vehicle Trials. By August 1907 a Wolseley-BTH omnibus had been put into service by the L.G.O.C. on its route between Barnes and Canning Town after completing about 5,000 miles as a demonstrator. Whilst in service with the L.G.O.C., all the electrical equipment was sealed and kept locked and only attended to by a B.T.H. service engineer. In January 1908 this bus was withdrawn from service after completing 13,390 miles, the last 3,470 miles of which had been completed without any stoppages for repairs, and completly stripped down at the Cricklewood garage to check for wear.

By December 1907 the company had outstanding orders for £400,000 worth of vehicles and equipment and the total workforce at the Crayford and Adderley Park works was 3,200 men.

In the following year, 1908, five more patents were applied for,

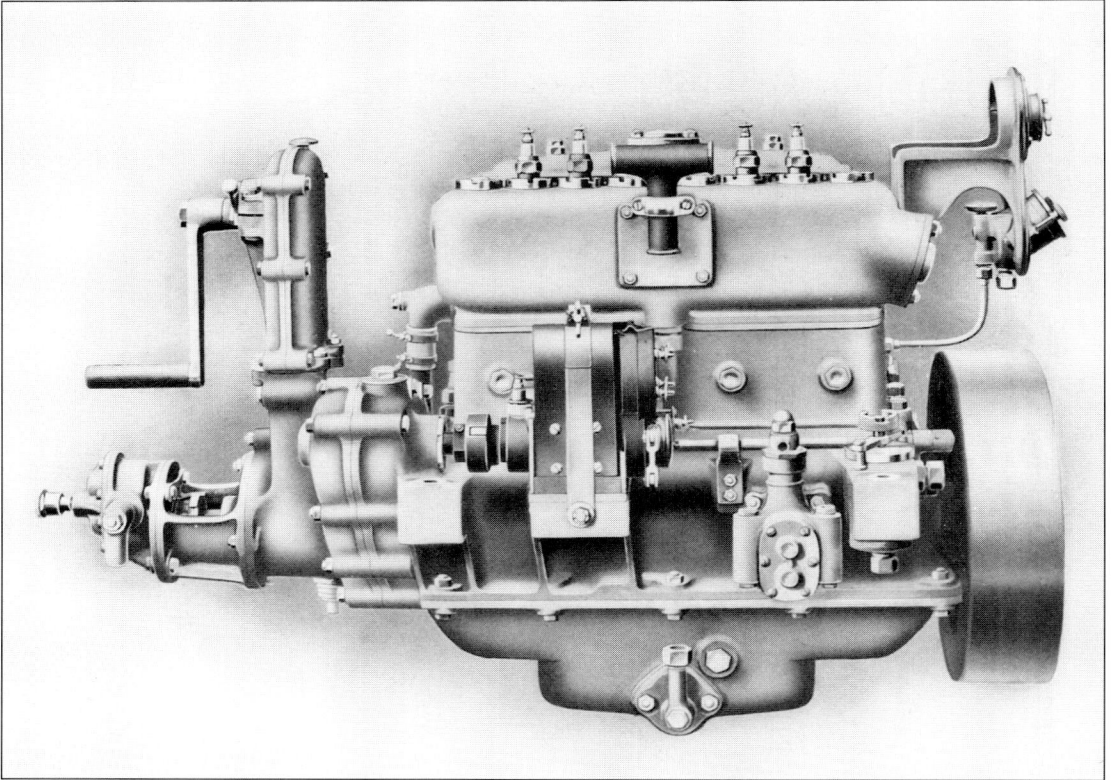

Two marine engines at opposite ends of the power spectrum, but both specifically designed to meet the arduous conditions encountered in marine installations.

TOP: A 4 cylinder 12 h.p. petrol engine with a bore of 3.125" diameter, stroke of 4.75", capacity of 2.38 litres, and with a power output of 5 b.h.p./litre. With a cast iron monobloc cylinder block, and cast iron pistons, the engine weighed 4.75 cwts, less the 14" diameter flywheel.

Starting was by the hand cranking handle at the front of the engine, and ignition was via a Bosch H.T. magneto. The engine had overall installation dimensions of 45" long by 30" high by 23.25" wide, and in 1912 cost £115, or £165 complete with factory built reversing gear.

BOTTOM: An excellent view of one of the 360 h.p. in-line 12 cylinder marine engines specially built for the Duke of Westminster's new Fauber Hydroplane, "Brunhilde", in 1911. It is believed that these engines had a bore of 7.25" diameter and stroke of 7.5", giving a capacity of 60 litres, and by present day standards they were quite lightly stressed developing about 5.9 h.p./litre.

From other pictures showing the actual engine installation it would appear that the engines were built 'handed', with their exhaust manifolds, and all parts requiring adjustment, to the outside, to give the most compact installation possible. One gets the impression that this engine design could have come from the drawing board of Arthur Rowledge, as this type of design was undoubtedly his forte.

At this time the largest production marine engine being offered by the company was a 180 h.p. in-line 8 cylinder with a bore of 6.5" diameter, stroke of 7", a capacity of 30.4 litres, developing its maximum power at 1,000 r.p.m., and cost £1,500. Ignition was via H.T. magneto with an auxiliary coil ignition of the Bosch dual type. The pistons were of high grade cast iron and lubrication was via a pump driven by a gear from the camshaft. The cylinder/head water jackets were made from planished copper sheets screwed and jointed to the cylinder blocks. All the marine engines were final bench tested for 4 hours, and were guaranteed to develop their quoted output.

numbers 108, 5542, 17807, 18149 and 24975, covering subjects such as, carburettors, engine lubrication and cooling, clutches and rear axle suspension. The latter, number 18149, shows a form of cantilever rear suspension which the company were to develop further and use extensively on their motor cars right into the 1920's.

In February 1908 two 200 h.p. 8 cylinder marine engines were built for a racing motor launch being developed jointly with Saunders & Co., who had a yard at East Cowes. The launch was named "Wolseley-Siddeley" and during races held at Monaco during the following month it achieved three wins and a fastest time. One race over 50 kilometres was covered at an average speed of 53.3 k.p.h. and a top speed of over 55 k.p.h. was recorded. The fuel consumption of these 8 cylinder engines is not known, but with petrol retailing at 1s-1d per gallon in Britain the cost of running such a craft would still have been appreciable. The launch was later sold to the Duke of Westminster who raced it at Monaco in April and set up a new World Record for the 100 km. race at an average speed of 39.12 m.p.h. Renamed "Ursula", the boat outclassed all the competition in the first race at Kiel the following year, so much so, that no competitors turned out for the second day of racing! In 1911 a new 15 metre Fauber Hydroplane was built for the Duke powered by two in-line 12 cylinder Wolseley engines each developing 360 h.p., the engines having originally been developed for "Ursula"

Marine engines were to become an important part of the company's range of products and by 1918 encompassed 4 cylinder, 6 cylinder and 8 cylinder petrol engines, in a range from a little over 1 litre up to 22 litres. A total of 10 marine engines was then available with 4 cylinder units of 1.06 litres (7 h.p.), 2.37 litres (12 h.p.), 3.07 litres (18 h.p.), 4.21 litres (24 h.p.), and 15.2 litres (80 h.p); 6 cylinder engines of 4.96 litres (30 h.p.), 10 litres (60 h.p.), and 22.8 litres (130 h.p.) and, interestingly, two lightweight V8 engines of 7.9 litres (72 h.p.) and 17.9 litres (140 h.p.) The largest of the 4 cylinder engines had a bore of 6.5" diameter and stroke of 7", weighed 14 cwts and cost £550 and the largest 6 cylinder engine had the same bore/stroke dimensions, but weighed 16.5 cwts and cost £1,100. (The latter engine was also available complete with reversing gear at a cost of £1,347-10s-6d) The two V8 engines were probably of aluminium and cast iron construction and had bore and stroke dimensions of 3.75" diameter by 5.5" and 5" diameter by 7" respectively and cost £550 and £1,210. By 1920 the range of marine engines had been reduced to about four models which included 4 cylinder models of 7 h.p. and 18 h.p. and 6 cylinder models of 32 h.p. and 60 h.p. The four cylinder models had a bore and stroke of 62mm diameter by 89mm and 90mm diameter by 120mm respectively, the bare engines weighing 1.75 cwts and 5.75 cwts and cost £160 and £325. The 6 cylinder engines had a bore and stroke of 90mm diameter by 130mm and 120mm diameter by 146mm respectively and weighed 7.5 cwts and 12 cwts. The 6 cylinder engines cost £400 and £750, or £510 and £900 if ordered complete with reversing gear and for an extra £20 or £50, respectively, could be equipped for running on paraffin.

The 10 h.p. motor cab introduced in 1907 had been joined by 12 h.p. and 18 h.p. models in 1908 and this mode of motor transport was becoming increasingly popular. In May 1908 the company

An Agreement

made this twenty second day of May One thousand nine hundred and eight 1Between The Wolseley Tool and Motor Car Company Limited of York Street in the City of Westminster (hereinafter called "The Wolseley Company") of the first part and Sydney Straker and Squire Limited of Nelson Square, Blackfriars, London, S.E. (hereinafter called the "Straker Company") of the second part, and Sidney Samuel Straker and Lionel Robert Littler Squire both of Nelson Square, aforesaid Managing Directors of the Straker Company (who and their respective executors and administrators are hereinafter referred to as "The Directors") of the third part Supplemental (First) to an agreement made between the Wolseley Company and the Straker Company dated the twenty first day of May One thousand nine hundred and six and (Secondly) to an agreement supplemental thereto of the same date and made between the same parties Whereas the Straker Company has agreed to purchase from the Wolseley Company One hundred and fifty engines for Motor Buses at a total price of Twenty seven thousand seven hundred and fifty pounds and eighty two of the said Engines have been delivered but the Straker Company has failed to take delivery of any further part thereof, And whereas no other orders by the Straker Company for engines or spare parts for Motor Buses are now pending And whereas the Straker Company was on the date hereof indebted to the Wolseley Company in the sum of Eighteen thousand one hundred and twenty two pounds seventeen shillings and three pence on current account in respect of the balance due on the Engines delivered and for the price of certain spare parts supplied to the Straker Company by the Wolseley Company and interest thereon as agreed (which account is hereinafter referred to as "Account 'A' ") and is also indebted in the further sum of Four thousand one hundred and forty two pounds nine shillings and seven pence being the agreed value of certain stock of spare parts manufactured by the Wolseley Company to meet the estimated requirements of the Straker Company or in connection with the manufacture of such of the Engines as have not yet been delivered And whereas by Special Resolution of the Straker Company duly passed and confirmed on the ninth and twenty fourth March One thousand nine hundred and eight it was resolved (inter alia) as follows:—

(1) That the two thousand unissued shares of One pound each in the capital of the Company numbered 10001 to 12000 inclusive, be consolidated in such a manner that every five of the said shares shall constitute one five pound share (2) That the shares resulting from such consolidation shall be preference shares and shall be numbered 10001 to 10400 inclusive so that the shares then representing those now numbered 10001 to 10,005

On May 21st 1906 the Sydney Straker & Squire Ltd., company of London, signed an agreement with the Wolseley Tool & Motor Car Co.Ltd., for Wolseley to supply them with 150 petrol engines for motor buses, at a total cost of £27,750. (The Straker company was actually in competition with Wolseley at this time to supply motor buses to London) Two years later, it would appear, Straker had not only broken the terms of this agreement by ordering only 82 of the 150 engines, but had also failed to make any payment to Wolseley for the engines, and spare parts, which had been an integral part of that agreement. The cost of the engines and spares, with interest on the sum which Straker had failed to pay, amounted to £18,122-17s-3d, plus a further £4,142-9s-7d, for spare parts manufactured by Wolseley in anticipation of the estimated demands required by Straker. One can imagine that some strongly worded exchanges had taken place between the two companies, concluding on 22nd May, 1908, by the signing of this new agreement, the first page of which is reproduced here.

Straker now agreed to transfer to Wolseley 3,000 £5 shares in the Straker company as a £15,000 payment towards the total amount owed, plus £250 per month, from the 31st May, 1908, until the debt had been cleared. Non payment of the agreed monthly sum would then make the whole sum of the debt payable immediately.

Futhermore, Wolseley also made Straker agree to apply to the Wolseley Tool & Motor Car Co.Ltd., first for all their motor bus engines, for buses of whatever size, or design, for the next 5 years. This gave Wolseley the first option of supplying Straker with engines, and gave them 7 days to decide whether they wanted Straker's business, or not, as they saw fit at the time.

It would appear that Straker succeeded in paying off the debt, otherwise the company would have gone into liquidation with Wolseley at the top of their creditors list, but it is not known how many more engines, if any, were actually supplied to Sydney Straker & Squire Ltd., by Wolseley.

announced that it had received orders for 250 10 h.p. cabs for the London General Motor Cab Company, 250 12 h.p. cabs for London United and an order for 100 long wheelbase 18 h.p. cabs for the London Provincial Cab Company. Production of cabs at Adderley Park East Works was running at 34 per week and the Crayford Works, which by this time was only building 18 h.p. chassis for private cars and cabs, was building 20 chassis per week. The 12 h.p. cab was reported to be giving excellent service returning 27/28 m.p.g. and using lubricating oil at about 350 m.p.g. This model was powered by a 2 cylinder vertical engine, had a three speed gearbox, 8ft 8ins wheelbase and cost £235 in chassis form. In February 1909 the Provincial Motor Cab Co., started a cab business in Birmingham with six Wolseley cabs and planned to increase the fleet to twenty. A taxi drivers strike in Birmingham later in the year was settled by the simple expedience of sacking them all and signing up a new batch of drivers!

The commercial vehicle range had been reduced drastically for 1908 and consisted of a 8 cwt van powered by a 2 cylinder 10 h.p. vertical engine, with a three speed gearbox and live rear axle priced at £298 in chassis form; a 30 cwt van/lorry powered by a 18 h.p. 4 cylinder vertical engine, three speed gearbox and live rear axle priced at £450 and a 3½ tons semi-forward control lorry powered by a 30 h.p. 4 cylinder engine, four speed gearbox, but with chain drive to the rear wheels, priced at £700. It is difficult to understand why, having spent so much time developing the commercial vehicle range, including the seemingly popular omnibus chassis which had been developed into a reliable vehicle, that the company suddenly cut back their range and concentrated on private motor cars again.

Mr. J.D.Siddeley was elected Hon. Treasurer of the Society of Motor Manufacturers & Traders in May and in August the company announced that a total of 298 cars had been built at the Adderley Park works during June and July.

In 1908, Birmingham, "an island isolated from the autocar", boasted a total of 1,606 private motor cars, 206 trade motor vehicles, 43 public carriages and 1,796 motor bicycles registered in the city.

Prices for Wolseley-Siddeley motor cars were, £250 in chassis form or £300 for a complete 10 h.p. model seating 2 or 4 passengers on a 7ft 6ins wheelbase chassis; £320 in chassis form or £380 for a 4 seater 14 h.p. model based on a 8ft 9ins wheelbase chassis; £500 in chassis form or £575 for a complete 18 h.p. car based on a 9ft 9ins wheelbase chassis; £550 in chassis form or £625 for a 5 seater 30 h.p. car based on a 9ft 6ins wheelbase chassis and £750 in chassis form or £875 for a complete 40 h.p. car based upon a 11ft 1in wheelbase chassis. A 40 h.p. model was also available on a 10ft 0in wheelbase chassis priced at £650 in chassis form only.

A 14 h.p. four cylinder engine was the subject of an observed bench test at the Crayford Works in September 1908 where the engine was run on a test bed at 1,600 r.p.m. for 20 minutes and was shown to be developing 40.85 b.h.p., and was then run at 2,000 r.p.m. for a period of five minutes when it developed 46.2 b.h.p.

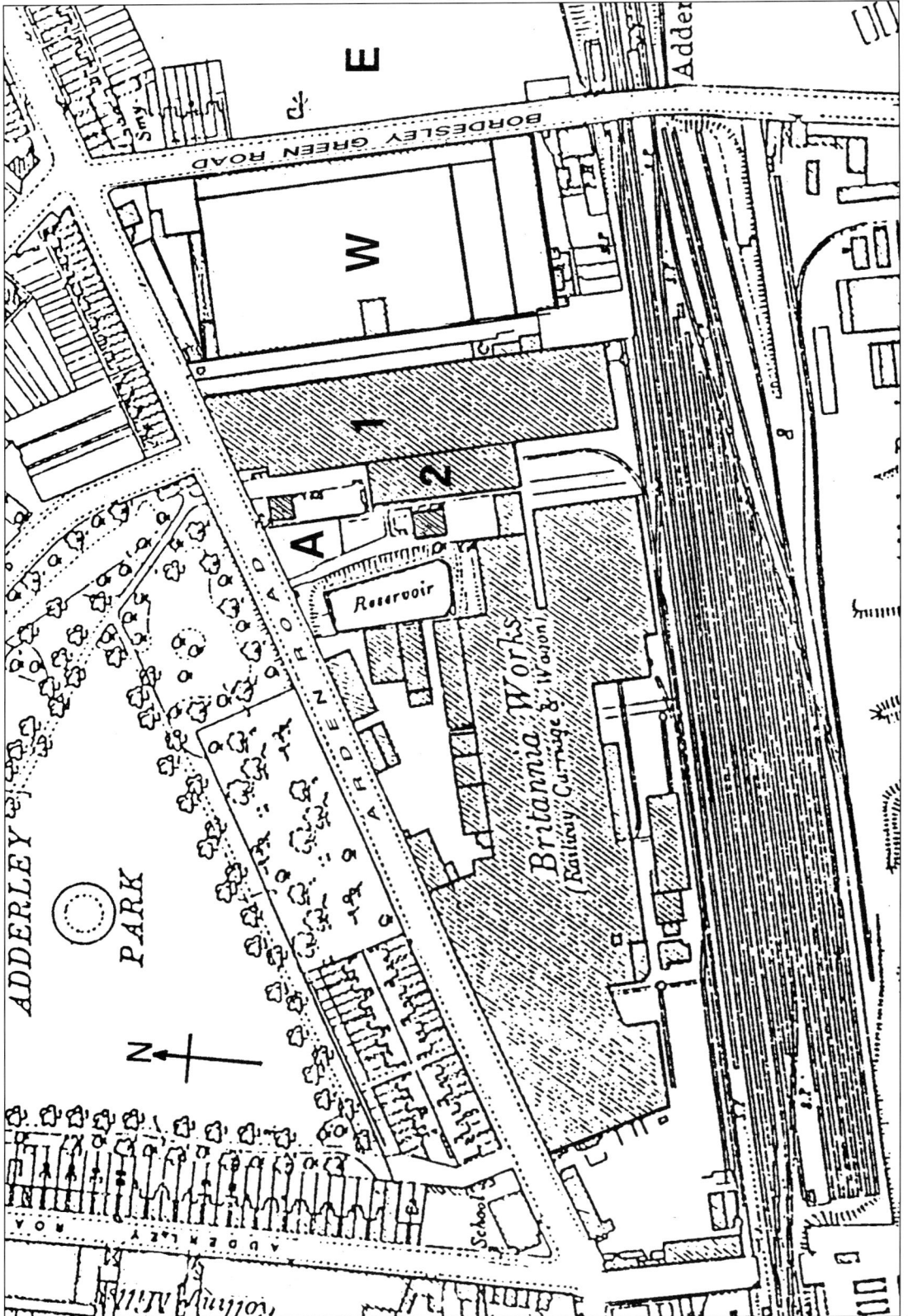

In 1909 the Adderley Park works was to expand rapidly into buildings adjacent to the West Works, known as the Britannia Works, which had hitherto been occupied by the railway carriage and waggon builder Brown, Marshalls & Company Limited who, since 1883, had progressively developed the site from the junction of Arden Road and Adderley Road, west of the Wolseley factory, upto the boundary of the original Starley Brothers & Westwood works in Bordesley Green Road. The first evidence of this expansion into the Britannia Works is given in a planning application, dated March 1909, when permission was sought to build toilets in what was described as a "new shop". This particular building, the old Iron Underframe Shop, which was immediately behind the single storey group of workshops (16 to 22 on the Starley Brothers & Westwood factory drawing) was 112 feet wide by 476 feet long, covering 1.2 acres, and against its west wall was a smaller building described as a Repair Shop which measured 72 feet by 196 feet, the latter having been constructed in 1900 and known as the 'Dew Wagon Shop'.

The only commercial vehicle available in the 1909 range of vehicles was a 30 cwts model powered by a 25 h.p. four cylinder engine with a bore of 4" diameter and stroke of 4½", priced at £502 and the 5 seater cab fitted with a two cylinder 12 h.p. engine and 3 speed gearbox was being offered for £380. For the 1909 season the motor car range had been extended again to include 10 h.p., 14 h.p., 18 h.p., 20 h.p., 30 h.p., 40 h.p. and 50 h.p. models, the 10 h.p. model having a 2 cylinder engine, the 20 h.p. and 50 h.p. models having 6 cylinder engines with the other models having 4 cylinder engines. All had bevel final drives with the strange exception of the 40 h.p. models which retained chain drive. The 10 h.p. model was based on a 8'-0" wheelbase chassis priced at £260; the 14 h.p. model was based on a 8'-9" wheelbase chassis at £330; the 18 h.p. model was based on a 9'-9" wheelbase chassis at £450; the 20 h.p. model was based on a 10'-0" wheelbase chassis at £575; the 30 h.p. model was based on a 10'-0" wheelbase chassis at £600; the 40 h.p. model was available on a 10'-0" or 11'-1" wheelbase chassis at £650 or £675 and the 50 h.p. model was based on a 11'-3" wheelbase chassis at £850. By this time the company was building 45 motor cars per week.

At the Aero & Motor Boat Show at Olympia that year the company displayed a 90° V8 water cooled aero engine with a bore of 90mm diameter and stroke of 125mm giving a capacity of 6.36 litres, which developed 60 b.h.p. at 1,350 r.p.m. and was fitted with twin Bosch magnetos. A straight 8 vertical engine for airships was also displayed which had a bore of 165mm diameter, stroke of 178mm, a capacity of 30.45 litres and developed 200 b.h.p. at 1,000 r.p.m.

In May the company announced that their vehicles would be called Wolseley-Siddeley to emphasize their origin from the Wolseley factory, instead of Siddeley's as they were more commonly referred to in the press and in June Mr.J.D. Siddeley resigned from the company and was appointed joint Managing Director of The Deasly Motor Car Manufacturing Company. One can only summise that there was a connection between these two announcements, but it would appear that the ambitious Siddeley was not amused!

DIAGRAM

This map shows the Adderley Park Works 'W' of Wolseley in 1903 and with the buildings of the Britannia Works of Brown, Marshalls & Company Ltd., shown shaded.

The areas numbered 1 and 2 were the first buildings of the Britannia Works to be taken over by Wolseley in 1909, the largest building (1) itself covered 1.2 acres and was destined to become an Assembly Shop and Forging Shop. The second building (2) was to become the Plating Shop.

The area 'A' between building number 1 and the boundary of the reservoir was referred to as Arden Works in some of the Wolseley drawings and is shown here with the two private houses close to building number 2, one of which had originally housed the Works Manager of Brown, Marshalls & Company Ltd. This area was to be redeveloped to house Engine Assembly Shops and Engine Test Houses.

Area 'E' in Bordesley Green Road had previously been occupied by the Parkfield Brick Company, but had been abandoned and eventually became the East Works of the Wolseley company.

LEFT: Both of these pictures show the Chassis Erection Shop, about 1910, when most of the vehicle assembly was taking place in building 'Bm' in the "Britannia Works". Unlike today the assembly of motor cars was done very much on an individual basis with the bare chassis frames supported by wooden trestles whilst a small team of workmen built up an entire car themselves. The amount of actual 'fitting' which took place can be judged by all the work benches where sub assembly of components would take place, together with hand finishing of items to get that perfect fit. Overseeing the workers were the 'gaffers' in their clean collars and ties, one of whom can be seen to the right of the top picture, almost standing to attention for the camera!

BELOW: No scantily clad girls here on the Wolseley stand at the 1909 Olympia Motor Show. The exhibits included two chassis, to show all the working bits, and with the chassis frames themselves so highly polished that they look like mirrors.

At the end of 1909 two new motor cars were announced, a 12/16 h.p. model with 4 cylinder engine and a 40/50 h.p. model with a 6 cylinder engine. Both of these new engines were of monobloc construction, i.e. the cylinders and crankcases were cast in a single unit, unlike previous Wolseley engines which had separate crankcase and cylinder block castings.

The great diversification of the company's products is well illustrated by the ten patents taken out in 1909, numbers 3453, 5129, 6038, 9923, 15805, 15806, 19315, 20061, 25623 and 28673, which cover internal combustion engines, carburettors, drives for aeroplanes, motor car hoods and airships. Patent number 6038 describes the design of a vee type aircraft engine where the drive for the propeller is taken from gearing also used to drive the camshaft. This design was used extensively by the company in the production of aero engines before and during the First World War. Patent number 15805 deals with pressure scavenged four stroke engines which relied on cylinder ports for inlet and exhaust and this idea is also covered again in patent number 28673.

The patent dealing with airships was taken out by Alfred Remington and the Naval Construction Works of Vickers, Sons & Maxim Ltd., in Barrow in Furness. It deals specifically with a device which maintains the weight of an airship during flight to compensate for the fuel being consumed to power its engines. The company had been involved with airships since about 1909 with the ill fated "Mayfly", which was powered by Wolseley engines, and the company were to be employed in the manufacture and testing of airship equipment for some years to come.

PHOTOGRAPHS

TOP: This unusual looking machine was a motor car chassis converted to take a V8 water cooled aero engine and used for test purposes. The aero engine can be seen to the rear of the chassis, together with its own fuel tank mounted high above the driver and the test engineer facing rearwards.

Expansion into the Britannia Works in 1910 continued with great vigour and by August it is clear that the Chassis Erecting Shop, Plating Shop, Smiths Shop, Aluminium Foundry, Carriage Smiths and Sawmill had all been re-located into the new works. With the acquisition of the Britannia Works the Wolseley factory now covered about 21 acres and was to expand further during 1915. A small pocket of land in Arden Road contained a water reservoir about 83 feet by 166 feet together with two private residences which had become surrounded by the Britannia Works. This land too was eventually to become part of the Wolseley factory and known as the Arden Works. In July 1910 the Experimental Shop was relocated into a building 58 feet 4inches by 100 feet overlooking the reservoir and gardens and a short distance from the Plating Shop.

In the East Works a two storey Mess Room was built, at a cost of £2,000, close to the row of houses at the north end of the site in Bordesley Green Road. The Mess Room was opened one hour before the factory was due to start work each day, to provide breakfasts for the ever expanding workforce which numbered some 4,000 men. This building eventually became the Staff Canteen in the days of Morris Commercial Cars Ltd.

Over 1,000 cars were produced in 1910 and with the adoption of metrication for engine building the car types were all redesignated to become, 12/16 h.p., 16/20 h.p., 20/28 h.p., 24/30 h.p., 30/34 h.p., 40 h.p., 40/50 h.p. and 50 h.p. For the first time in the company's history a two cylinder engined car was dropped from its range and with the exception of the 24/30 h.p. and 50 h.p. 6 cylinder models all the new models had four cylinder engines with a mixture of bevel or worm final drive rear axles.

The 12/16 model was the only car to retain a three speed gearbox, was based on a 9'-0" wheelbase chassis and cost £310 in chassis form; the 16/20 model was available on a 9'-5" or 10'-1" wheelbase chassis costing £395 or £420; the 20/28 model too was available on either a 10'-0" or 10'-6" wheelbase chassis costing £510 or £535; the 24/30 model had a 10'-9" wheelbase chassis and cost £610; the 30/34 model had a 10'-6" wheelbase and cost £550; the 40/50 model had an 11'-0" wheelbase chassis and cost £675 and the top of the

BOTTOM-LEFT: A general view of just part of the Body Shop situated in the "Britannia Works". At this time, 1910, body building was being undertaken here and in the East Works, but it would be in the "Britannia Works" where, 4 years later, production of ambulances and military vehicles would be concentrated.

BELOW: Built in 1910 as a private omnibus this Wolseley was powered by a 4 cylinder 18 h.p. engine mounted vertically under the floor at the front of the vehicle. Fitted with pneumatic tyres on the front and solid tyres on the rear it was capable of carrying eleven passengers in the enclosed rear compartment, together with their luggage on the roof rack.

LEFT: (BMIHT photo) One of the sleighs built for Scotts Antarctic Expedition standing in building '4d' in the East Works. The side covers have been removed to show the 4 cylinder engine and, if you follow the pipework, you will see that the rudimentary drivers seat was heated by the exhaust system as was the carburettor.

BOTTOM-LEFT: A large 4 cylinder engine being coupled up to an electric dynamometer used for performance testing of engines. This form of dynamometer could be 'loaded' electrically to impose various loads on the engine under test so that its performance could be evaluated under all conditions and speeds. The company used Monte-Callow electric engine dynamometers and Heenan & Froude water dynamometers of various capacities.

BELOW: General view of one of the Engine Test Houses which were situated in building 'Bv' of the Britannia Works', this particular building housing 40 test beds. There were no dynamometers in this building to test engine performance, so this test house was probably used to 'run-in' engines, correct settings and cure leaks, etc., before passing them to another test house for full performance testing. The average time taken to complete a full engine test was 3 days! This can be more readily understood when it is known that the engines were run initially on town gas for half of the test procedure, after which they would be stripped completely and examined to ensure that everything was correct, before being re-assembled and run on petrol for the remainder of the test procedure.

range 50 h.p. model was available on a chassis with a wheelbase of 11'-7" for £1,000.

A total of six patents were applied for in 1910, numbers 5431, 6311, 9334, 13573, 16783 and 30340, covering internal combustion engines, carburettors, radiators and suspension. Patent 16783 covered the design of a sleeve valve engine and an engine fitted with a duplex piston valve for controlling inlet and exhaust ports.

Wolseley designed and built three special motorised sleighs in 1910 for Captain Scotts Antarctic Expedition, the sleighs being powered by 12 h.p. four cylinder air cooled petrol engines with carburettors heated by the exhaust system. A gearbox with two forward gears gave speeds of 2 m.p.h. and 3½ m.p.h., and gradient ability of 1 in 2, the drive from the gearbox being taken to a worm drive axle with chain drive to the caterpillar tracks. The sleighs were tested in Norway before being loaded onto a ship bound for New Zealand where they were transhipped on board the "Terra Nova" for shipment to the Antarctic. Unfortunately, one of the sleighs was lost whilst being unloaded and remains to this day in the frozen waters of McMurdo Sound. About a year later two similar sleighs were built for the German Antarctic Expedition. The sleighs were to be of little use to Scott, as they proved to be incapable of traversing the rough ice blocks without becoming stuck, or falling over, due to the lack of articulation in the simple track design.

In May Mr Arthur McCormack, who had previously been the Technical Manager, was appointed Managing Director to replace Mr Ernest Hopwood who had been Managing Director since August 1909. In September 1910 the parent company Vickers announced that they had developed a new metal which they called "Duralumin", but although it was thought Wolseley would be the first company to use the new material it was the Electric & Ordnance Accessories Co.Ltd., a subsidiary of Vickers, with a factory called "Stellite Works" in Cheston Road, Aston, Birmingham, who

LEFT-TOP: This Assembly Shop was situated in building 'Wk' of the "Britannia Works" which had previously been a wagon Iron Underframe Shop in the days of Brown, Marshalls & Co.Ltd.,. The main component being assembled here was the steering gear comprising the column, steering box with gears and aluminium steering wheel covered in leather. The main impression gained from this picture is how labour intensive the motor car industry was in those early days.

BOTTOM: A close up view taken in the large Aluminium Foundry showing engine crankcase moulds being made in pneumatically operated sand moulding machines. Steel cores were often used to produce the moulds instead of the more widely used wooden cores, as these were considered to provide more accurate moulds/castings.

BELOW: A general view of the Aluminium Foundry where engine crankcases, sumps, steering wheels and other small aluminium castings were produced. The size of this building and the spacing of the roof supports would suggest that this picture was taken when the foundry was situated in the "Britannia Works", building 'Bp'.

first exhibited parts made from "Duralumin" at the Olympia Show in November of the same year. This company had been established some time and manufactured the Warner 'Autometer', universal joints, Timken bearings and the Hall dual ignition system and were later to produce motor car wheels, front axles and rear axles with worm or bevel gear drives. Wolseley adopted the use of Timkin bearings in some of their rear hubs during 1910 and were to become inextricably associated with the Electric & Ordnance Accessories company within a few years.

The import/export figures for 1910 showed that 4,518 complete cars and 6,551 chassis had been imported into Britain at a cost of £3,111,555 and 3,569 complete motor cars and 562 chassis had been exported worth £1,593,568. In 1911 no less than 19 patents were applied for dealing with internal combustion engines, carburettors, motor car hoods, gearboxes and suspension. The patents were numbers, 633, 634, 983, 1421, 1762, 2566, 2568, 3892, 11578, 16389, 16879, 17651, 20288, 20959, 21199, 24316, 25419, 25421 and 26565. Patent number 16879 deals with improvements to the rear axle suspension employing cantilever type road springs, and 25421, taken out jointly by Remington and Rowledge, deals with various designs of independent front suspension based around a transverse leaf spring. Although the designs appeared to offer effective control of the front wheels, whilst giving improved ride and handling qualities, none found their way into production motor cars.

The Britannia Works continued to be developed in 1911 with the construction of a new Iron Foundry 50 feet wide by 220 feet long which was 28 feet 3 inches high to the eaves and 43 feet high overall, which would lead to the closure of the iron foundry located in the West Works close to the Bordesley Green Road.

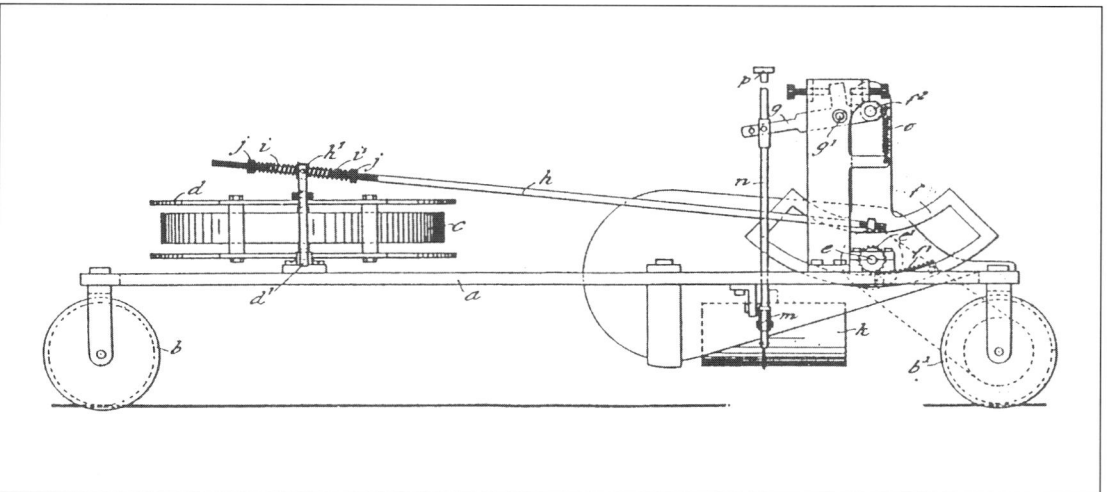

STRANGER THAN FICTION?

TOP: (BMIHT photo).The Gyrocar in chassis form, probably taken during the early stages of development as it is fitted with a board mounted on planks to form a crude seat for the brave driver who had to carry out testing. Comparing this picture with the one below of the completed car the reader will see that a major redesign of the front wheel steering geometry and suspension took place, but the vehicle still proved to be difficult to steer around corners without falling over!

CENTRE: The completed Gyrocar, which seated five passengers plus the driver, out on test near the Adderley Park works and fitted with company trade plates. The gentleman seated next to the driver is Peter Schilowsky the Russian inventor. The sight of this very strange looking vehicle travelling along the road must have caused quite a stir amongst pedestrians only just getting accustomed to four wheeled motor cars.To prevent the car falling over when coming to rest, or if the engine stalled, large sprags were fitted each side of the vehicle which could be lowered by hand in cases of emergency.

In 1924 Schilowsky admitted that the Gyrocar had not been the success he had hoped, as it had been built much too heavy and there had been serious problems in turning tight corners because of the centrifugal effect of the gyro-scope flywheel which weighed 600 lbs.

DRAWING

Part of the drawing from Peter Schilowsky's patent, number 12021, covering the basic principles of controlling a two wheeled vehicle by a gyroscope, which led to the building of the Wolseley Gyrocar in 1912. At the time of applying for this patent Schilowsky was living in Honor Oak, London.

The chassis frame is represented by (a) in the illustration, where a gyroscope (c) is mounted on two pivots (d) and the road wheels are (b) and (b). A pendulum (k) is free to swing transversely across the chassis frame and through various levers, a fulcrum and rack arrangement, inclinations of the vehicle are transmitted to the gyroscope mountings in the form of pulses to which the gyroscope reacts about its mountings causing corrections to be made to the inclination of the vehicle chassis. The patent also mentions that a hand operated lever could also be provided to operate the mechanism which generated impulses to the gyroscope, to give manual control of the vehicle.

In 1912 one of the strangest vehicles ever to emerge from a British motor car factory was built at the Adderley Park Works. The vehicle was a two wheeled car capable of carrying up to six people, driven by a 20 h.p. petrol engine and kept upright by a gyroscope revolving at 1,200 to 1,500 r.p.m. mounted beneath the centre seats. The car, which weighed 3 tons, had been designed by a Russian inventor, Peter Schilowsky, Governor of Kostroma, who specialised in the design of gyroscopically controlled vehicles including mono track rail cars. In fact, Schilowsky had demonstrated a steam powered model mono-rail car locomotive at the Westminster Palace Hotel in May 1910.

The 'Gyrocar' was tested around the Adderley Park works and demonstrated around London in March 1914. The rear wheel was driven via a standard Wolseley motor car gearbox, but when the car was demonstrated in London the gear ratios were found to be too high and a special set of reduction gears were made to give the car a top speed of about 12 m.p.h. The car was never shipped to Russia and was buried in the Wolseley works in Drews Lane, Birmingham. Some years later it was exhumed and cut up for scrap. Schilowsky continued to patent gyroscopically controlled vehicles into the 1920's and is believed to have died in Hereford in 1956.

However, this was not the first time Wolseley had been connected with a gyroscopically controlled vehicle, as the company had supplied a 20 h.p. engine and a 80 h.p. engine to a Mr. Louis Brennan in 1909 for a mono rail loco cum load carrier which was displayed at the Japan-British Exhibition in Shepherds Bush in June 1909. Brennan had built his mono rail vehicle in Gillingham, Kent, the vehicle resembling a large motor lorry, but with two pairs of wheels set one behind the other on the centre line of the vehicle which was 40 feet long, 10 feet wide, 13 feet high, weighed some 22 tons and could carry 10 tons. The 20 h.p. engine was connected to a dynamo which powered a motor driving two 15 cwt contra-rotating gyro flywheels which ran at 3,000 to 3,300 r.p.m. in a partial vacuum. The 80 h.p. engine also drove a dynamo supplying power to the main traction motor to propel the vehicle along the track.

The Britannia Works were developed further in 1912 when a large open yard 129 feet by 87 feet 6 inches, adjacent to the Chassis Erection Shop and Plating Shop, was roofed over to form additional workshop space. By this time the Chassis Erecting Shop had been equipped with "Prony" brake rigs which were used to test completed chassis before being passed to the Chassis Test Department for road testing. Each completed chassis would be reversed onto the rig where the rear axle would be clamped rigidly to part of the rig and the rear wheels would be removed and replaced by two large chain wheels. A chain would then be fitted between the "Prony" rig (which was something like an engine dynamometer) and each chain wheel and the motor car engine would then be started and tested at various speeds driving through the gearbox and rear axle. By knowing the power output of each type of model any drop in power or efficiency could be gauged by measuring equipment on the test rig which could point to problems in either the engine, gearbox or rear axle of the chassis under test. Only after completing this test and meeting the standards required would the chassis be passed

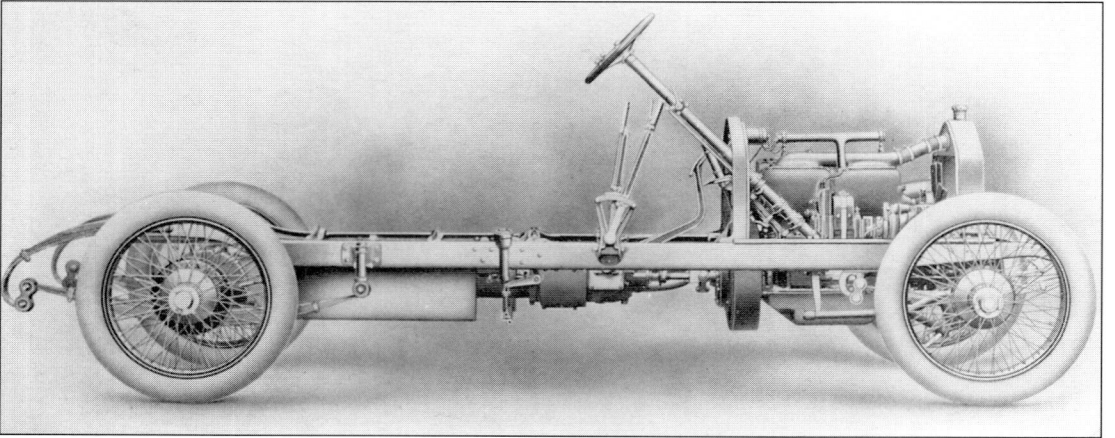

over to the Chassis Testing Department, in the East Works, where conventional road testing would be carried out.

On the East Works site a new temporary Body Stores was erected measuring 252 feet by 40 feet which was 12 feet high to the eaves and 23 feet high overall and the 15 feet wide space between the Smiths Shop and Upholstering & Paint Shop was roofed over. During 1912 £50,000 had been spent on additional plant to improve production of motor vehicles.

For the 1912 season there were, basically, six models, the 12/16 h.p., 16/20 h.p., 20/28 h.p., 24/30 h.p., 35/40 h.p. and the splendid top of the range 50 h.p. With the exception of the standard type 12/16 h.p. chassis all models were fitted with 4 speed gearboxes, and even the long wheelbase version of the 12/16 h.p. chassis also featured a 4 speed gearbox, leaving the baby of the family with a 3 speed gearbox. The 12/16 h.p. engine was a 4 cylinder monobloc design with a bore of 79mm diameter, stroke of 121mm and a capacity of 2,372 c.c. Ignition was by a Bosch H.T. magneto with variable timing (steering wheel control lever), although a dual ignition system was available for an extra £7-10s-0d. All the Wolseley motor car engines at this time were fitted with a combined oil/air pump, the latter being used to give a pressurised petrol supply from the petrol tank to the carburettor. On the standard 12/16 model the petrol tank was mounted beneath the drivers seat, but every other model in the range had the petrol tank mounted longitudinally inside the chassis frame.

A multi-plate clutch took the power to the 3 speed gearbox via a short open propshaft, then by an open propshaft to the underslung worm drive live rear axle with a ratio of 4.375:1. The braking system, common to all the 1912 cars, comprised a pedal operated metal to metal contracting band brake on the gearbox mounted drum, and internal expanding shoes in drums at each rear wheel operated by the hand lever mounted alongside the gear selector quadrant to the right hand side of the driver. The standard 12/16 model had a wheelbase of 9ft 3ins and front track of 4ft 1in, and the worm and sector steering gave a turning circle of 37ft. Suspension was by conventionally mounted semi-elliptic leaf springs, front and rear, with the rear of the rear springs connected by shackles to short extension brackets bolted to the sides of the chassis frame sidemembers. This model, in chassis form, cost £305. The long wheelbase version of the 12/16 had a wheelbase of 10ft 2ins and front track of 4ft 6ins. However, the chassis frame sidemembers on this model were swept downwards in front of the rear wheels to provide a lower floor line to the rear passenger compartment, and the rear suspension was changed to underslung semi-elliptic leaf springs coupled by shackles to the cantilevered end of half of a three quarter elliptic spring, inverted, and with its fixed end bolted to the chassis frame sidemember. The worm drive rear axle had a ratio of 5.142:1 and this model cost £335 in chassis form.

The 16/20 h.p. model had a 4 cylinder, cast in pairs, engine with a bore of 90mm diameter, stroke of 121mm and capacity of 3,079 c.c., and was fitted with dual ignition comprising a Bosch H.T. dual magneto and induction coil. The multi-plate clutch ran in oil and the rest of the mechanical specification followed that of the long wheelbase smaller model, but with a standard rear axle ratio of 4.11:1. However, this model was available with a choice of two wheelbases, 9ft 8ins or 10ft 4ins, both with a front track of 4ft

PHOTOGRAPHS

LEFT: All these photographs show models from the 1912 range of motor cars.

TOP: The 12/16 h.p. model was available in two wheelbase options, 9ft 3ins and 10ft 2ins and this picture shows the long wheelbase chassis with the frame sidemembers lowered just in front of the rear axle to allow better access into the passenger compartment of covered carriage bodywork. This chassis cost £335.

CENTRE: The chassis of the 20/28 h.p. model powered by a four cylinder 25.6 h.p. engine which had a bore of 102mm diameter and stroke of 130mm. This 10ft 9ins wheelbase chassis cost £490 and weighed 20 cwts.

BOTTOM: The Torpedo Touring Phaeton body mounted on a 24/30 h.p. six cylinder engine chassis with a wheelbase of 10ft 10ins. The 30.4 h.p. engine had a bore of 90mm diameter and stroke of 130mm and drove through a metal to metal multi-plate clutch into a four speed gearbox and bevel drive rear axle. In chassis form this model cost £600 and as a complete car, £809-3s-6d.

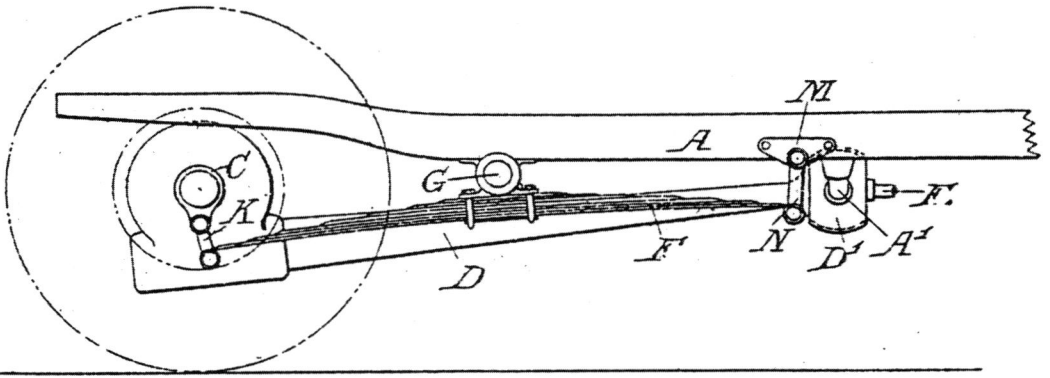

Fig.1

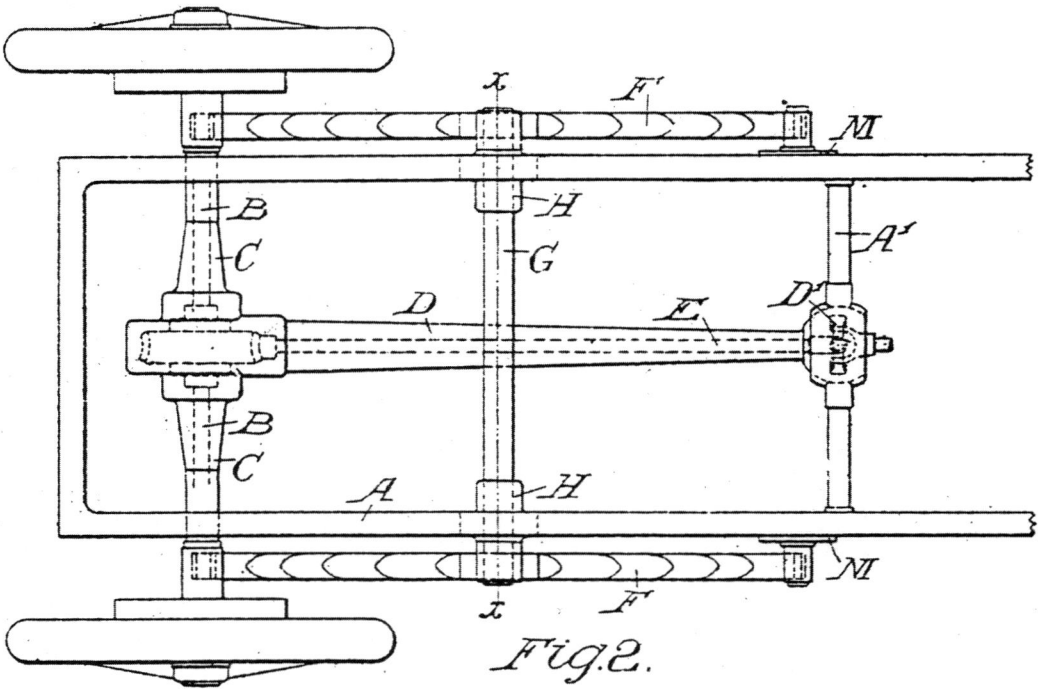

Fig.2.

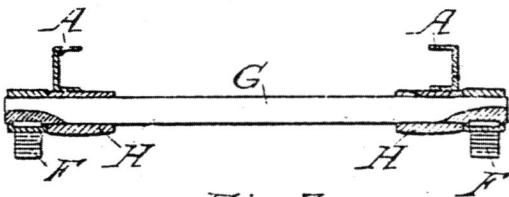

Fig.3.

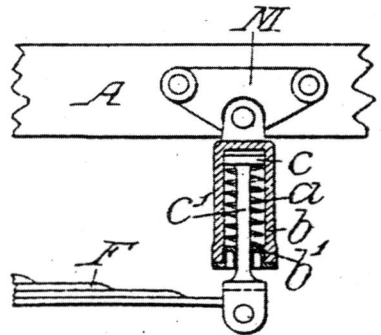

Fig.4.

4.5ins, the cost being £390 and £400, respectively.

The next model in the range, the 20/28 h.p., also had a 4 cylinder, cast in pairs, engine, with a bore of 102mm diameter, stroke of 130mm and capacity of 4,249 c.c. Rear axles now changed to live bevel gear types, with a standard ratio of 3.611:1 specified for open type bodies and 3.833:1 ratio axle for closed body models. Only available with one wheelbase of 10ft 9ins, these cars had a front track of 4ft 6ins, and cost £490 for open cars with 32" diameter road wheels, and £500 for closed cars fitted with 34" diameter road wheels.

The smallest of the 6 cylinder models, with cylinders cast in pairs, was the 24/30 h.p. model, the engine having a bore of 90mm diameter, stroke of 130mm, capacity of 4,962 c.c., and RAC rating of 30.4 h.p. The front suspension on this model was by conventionally mounted semi-elliptic leaf springs, but this model, like the other remaining models in the range, had a 3 spring design to the rear axle comprising conventional axle mounted semi-elliptics coupled by their rear shackles to the cantilevered ends of an inverted, transversely mounted, semi-elliptic leaf spring, which had its centre bolted to a tubular extension of the main chassis frame. This suspension design was quite popular in the 19th century as the rear suspension of horse drawn carts and carriages, but obviously had considerable merit in its application to Wolseley motor cars which formed their top of the range models, and usually fitted with closed limousine type bodies. The chassis had a wheelbase of 10ft 10ins, front track of 4ft 6ins, and cost £600. Largest of the 4 cylinder engined chassis was the 35/40 h.p. model, built on the 10ft 10 ins wheelbase chassis frame, which had a bore of 121mm diameter, stroke of 130mm, capacity of 5,980 c.c., and with a RAC rating of 36.1 h.p. The bevel drive rear axle had a standard ratio of 3.22:1, giving the car a top speed of about 48 m.p.h. and this 23 cwts chassis cost £600.

Top of the Wolseley range was the 50 h.p. 6 cylinder model, the engine having a bore of 114mm diameter, stroke of 146mm and capacity of 8,942 c.c. The bevel drive rear axle had a ratio of 3.44:1, giving a top gear capability of 58 m.p.h. Available on a choice of two chassis frames, with wheelbases of 11ft 9ins or 12ft 3ins, these were suitable for the largest enclosed bodies available, and cost £1,000 in chassis form.

Like all the other Wolseley chassis available for 1912, the 50 h.p. rear suspension could be built to specifically suit the differing weights of various bodies, there being little in the way of compromise in the designs, and all models throughout the range were fitted with Rudge-Whitworth detachable wire wheels as standard. Bodies for the 12/16 h.p. included a 2 seater De-Luxe, 4 seat Flush Sided Phaeton, and Coupe's in the form of a Brougham and Landaulette, and costing between £85 and £140. For the long wheelbase 12/16 h.p. a Limousine Landaulette was available, with canopy and screen to the drivers compartment for £225 in Best Finish. For the 16/20 h.p. chassis a similar range of bodies to the 12/16 h.p. were available, plus a Torpedo Touring Phaeton, Limousine, Brougham, and Cabrio-Phaeton for the long wheelbase chassis. Bodies for the 24/30 h.p. and the 35/40 h.p. chassis included a Torpedo Touring Phaeton, Cabrio-Phaeton, Cabriolet, Limousine, Limousine Landualette and an Imperial Limousine, at prices from £140 to £280. With the exception of the Cabrio-Phaeton, all the above

ILLUSTRATION

Patent number 16879, taken out by Alfred Remington, virtually finialised the design of the Wolseley cantilever type rear suspension and was, in fact, the design in its most simple form. The rear axle was located by, and driven through, a torque tube which swivelled about the transverse crossmember (A). The outer ends of the rear axle casing were connected to the cantilever road springs through shackles(K). The road springs were bolted at their centres to a transverse shaft which was carried in mountings(H), the shaft being free to rotate on bearings. The front eyes of the road springs were connected to the chassis frame either through shackles(N), or via the coil spring device shown in Fig. 4. Small road surface oscillations were absorbed by the coil spring device and larger vertical movements were absorbed by the road springs rotating together about the transverse tube.

However, the whole theory of this design was to prevent excessive roll on cornering and this was achieved by the transverse tube which acted, in effect, like a giant torsion bar which prevented the suspension on one side from deflecting more than the other side and so preventing excessive roll on cornering. To carry out performance testing of their motor car suspension designs the company built a special test rig which resembled a modern rolling road, but with one large drum rotated by the wheel of the car being tested. A large 'sett' was bolted across the drum to deflect the wheel/suspension and a crude arrangement of probes and pens attached to the suspension provided a very rudimentary chart showing suspension movements.

A Wolseley Imperial Limousine.

WOLSELEY

SIDDELEY.

"THE CAR FOR COMFORT AND RELIABILITY."

"From the very earliest days of the Automobile industry, the Wolseley Co. has ever worked to produce the best class of chassis construction, has ever sought to maintain a reputation for reliability, and has ever upheld a dignified position in the van of progressive design."—*Automobile Journal.*

Send for Catalogue No. 15, *post free.*

THE WOLSELEY TOOL AND MOTOR CAR CO., LTD.

(Proprietors : VICKERS, SONS & MAXIM, Ltd.),

Telegrams :
"Exactitude, Birmingham." ADDERLEY PARK, BIRMINGHAM. Telephone :
6153 Central.

LONDON : York St., Westminster.
Telegrams · "Autovent, London."
Telephone · 831 Victoria (Garage 823 Westminster).

MANCHESTER : 76, Deansgate.
Telegrams : "Autocar, Manchester."
Telephone : 6995.

F223

LEFT: A 1910 advertisement for the Imperial Limousine. By 1912 this body could be had on the 35/40 h.p. and 50 h.p. chassis which cost £905-18s-6d and £1,305-18s-6d, respectively.

BELOW: This drawing shows the general layout of a 18 h.p. industrial Lighting Set, as offered by the company in 1910. The power unit was a 3.7 litre four cylinder engine with a bore of 4" diameter and stroke of 4½" which developed 20 b.h.p. at 900 r.p.m. The cylinder block could be specified in either cast iron or aluminium and the engine was mounted on a cast iron bedplate. The weight of the engine in cast iron was 6½ cwts, the flywheel alone weighing 1.25 cwts.

Water cooling was via a radiator and engine driven fan with a water pump driven by gears off the crankshaft. Although offered as standard with a petrol carburettor this unit could also be specified with a patented dual carburettor for petrol or paraffin. A purchaser, or his representative, could be present when the engine was tested to verify the engine performance which had a maximum output of 22 b.h.p. at 1,000 r.p.m. on petrol and 18 b.h.p. at 1,000 r.p.m. on paraffin.

bodies were available on 50 h.p. chassis at the same prices.

The company had its own customer insurance arrangements with Lloyds Policies with premiums from £9-15s-0d for a 12/16 h.p. model up to £27-18s-0d for a 50 h.p. Imperial Limousine. The cover included use on the Continent for up to two months, Medical Expenses for personal injuries up to £10-10s-0d and even free legal advice. A School of Motoring Instruction was also run by the company where "Owners or their Servants may go through a complete course of tuition, both in Driving and Theory." Started initially at its York Street premises in London tuition at the School of Motoring Instruction was also available at the Adderley Park works.

In November 1912 Remington announced plans for Wolseley to re-enter the commercial vehicle market with a new 25 cwt model to be known as the 'CC6'. With two wheelbase options of 10'-9" or 11'-3", the new model had a track of 4'-8½' and overall width of 5'-1½", was to be powered by a four cylinder 16/20 h.p. engine with a bore of 90mm diameter and stroke of 121mm and was fitted with a four speed gearbox. This change in policy was to reap considerable dividends and placed the company in a strong position to supply all types of commercial vehicles during the First World War.

No less than 14 patents were applied for in 1912 covering such subjects as engine valve gear, suspensions, aero engines and 'balancing vibrations in mechanisms'. The patent numbers were, 831, 1099, 1886, 2008, 2595, 4427, 8298, 9113, 9240, 17101, 18168, 25009, 25010 and 29207. Patent number 18168 is of particular interest as it deals with the design of air cooled vee type aero engines which had their exhaust valves surrounded by small water jackets which were connected to a small radiator placed between the propeller and the front of the engine. Apparently air cooled aero engines of the day suffered from exhaust valve seizure due to overheating and this invention was designed to cure the problem.

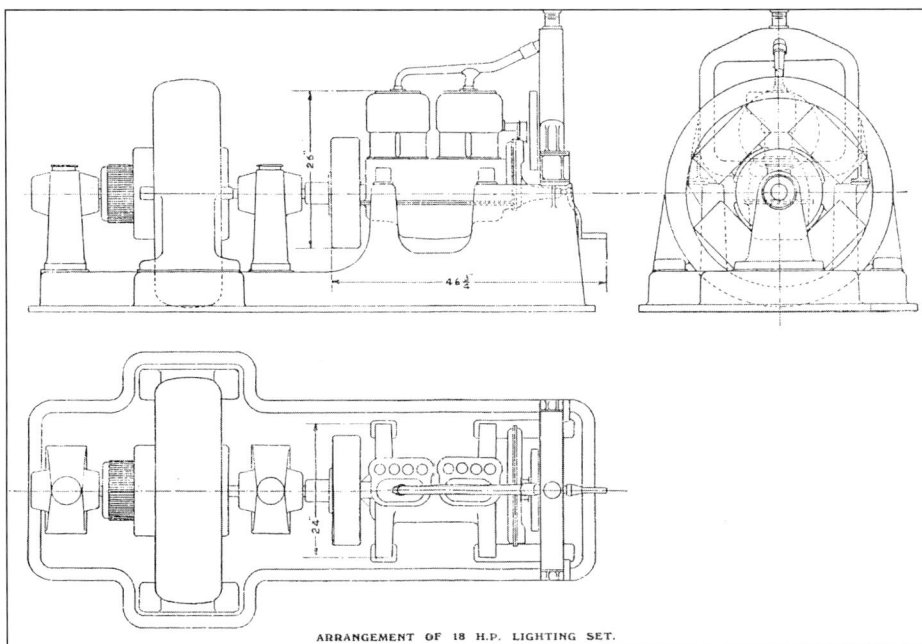

ARRANGEMENT OF 18 H.P. LIGHTING SET.

LEFT TOP: A 1912 Coupe Brougham 2 seater body fitted to a short wheelbase 16/20 h.p. chassis. The body itself cost £135 and a pair of headlamps complete with mounting brackets were available for an extra £14-15s-0d.

BOTTOM: A typical 1912 4 speed gearbox, with the cover removed to show the internal gearing, and with the foot pedal operated hinged band type brake shown clearly to the right hand side of the gearbox casing. The gearbox itself employed a remotely fitted change speed lever attached to the right hand side chassis frame sidemember.

BELOW: An interesting trio of Wolseley cars parked outside Battle Abbey, Sussex. The cars all belonged to Mr. M.P. Grace the owner of Battle Abbey, and are a 50 h.p. Limousine, a 24/30 h.p. open car and a 30 h.p. Shooting Brake which featured inward facing seats in the rear passenger compartment.

The company was still engaged in the production of aero engines and in 1912 built four such engines for the Italian Government. These water cooled V8's had a bore of 5" diameter and stroke of 7" giving a capacity of 18 litres and developing 120 b.h.p. with a specific fuel consumption of 0.655 pints/bhp-hr. Stringent testing of these engines was carried out including an 18 hour run at 1,150 r.p.m.

By January 1913 the plans to re-enter the commercial vehicle market had changed dramatically and a range consisting of 20 cwts, 25 cwts, 30 cwts and 35 cwts was to be made all powered by 16/20 h.p. engines and available as lorries, vans, mail vans, buses and char-a-bancs. One of the first customers to order some of the new Wolseley's was W.H. Smith, who took delivery of a closed van and a tilt van in February 1913. In July the company announced an extension to the commercial vehicle range with the addition of a 30 cwt and 3 ton model built in accordance with the War Office Subsidy specifications. To qualify for the War Office Subsidy Scheme vehicles had to be submitted to the Mechanical Transport Committee of the War Department for extensive trials to assess their suitability for military use should the need arise. The first part of these trials was conducted by the company over a three week period when the vehicles were expected to cover at least 200 miles per week. On completion of this 'running-in' the vehicles were handed over to the War Department for examination and were then subjected to final trials consisting of 18 daily runs of 80 to 90 miles per day, the testing all being carried out in the Aldershot and Woolwich areas. Three ton vehicles were expected to maintain an

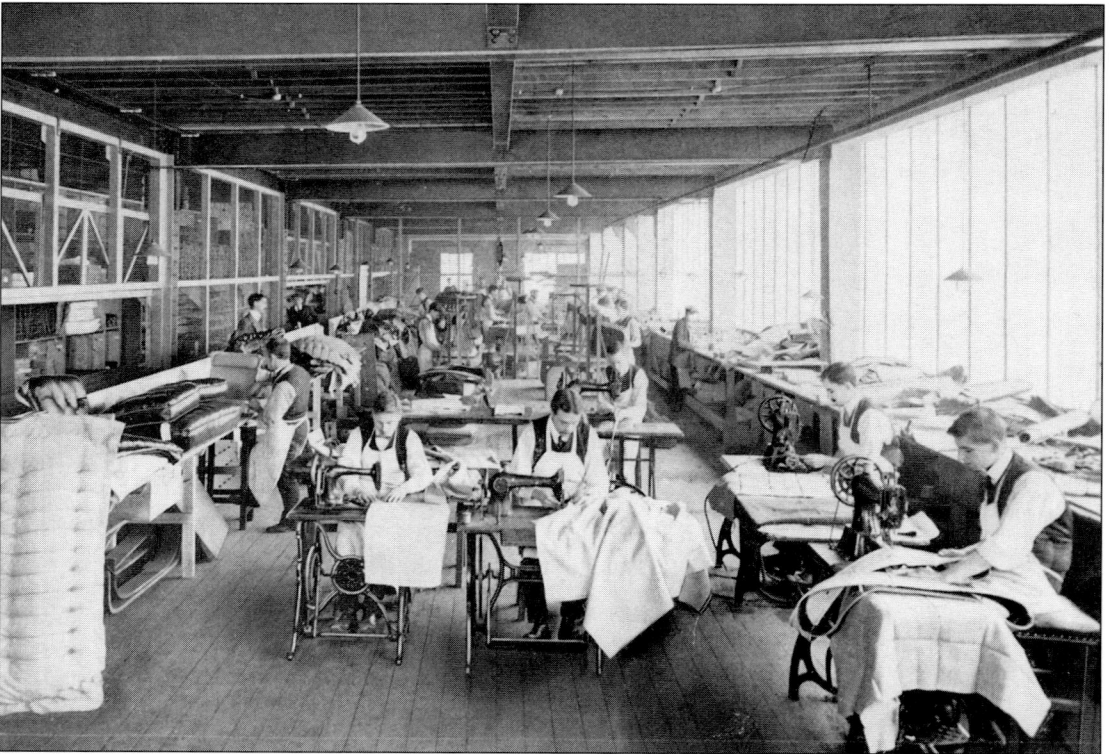

average speed of 12 m.p.h. on main roads and 10 m.p.h. on hilly routes and petrol consumption was expected to average at least 7 m.p.g. during testing. Test hills with gradients of 1 in 6 were negotiated and vehicles were expected to climb these several times from standing starts. Brake tests were also carried out on these hills, both in forward and reverse gears, with both the footbrake and handbrake required to hold the fully laden vehicles independently. Upon successful conclusion of all these trials the vehicles were taken into military workshops and stripped completely for examination. The Wolseley lorries passed these trials with flying colours the first time submitted and qualified easily for the War Department Subsidy Scheme. Shortly afterwards the published range of commercials included the 'CA' 12 cwts powered by a four cylinder 12/16 h.p. engine priced at £335; the 'CC' and 'CP' 20 cwts and 35 cwts models powered by a four cylinder 16/20 h.p. engine priced at £415 and £475 respectively; the 'CL' 40 cwts model powered by a four cylinder 20/28 h.p. engine priced at £610 and the 'CR' 70 cwts model powered by a four cylinder 35 h.p. engine and costing £725. However, the motor car range for 1913 had been trimmed back to just three models, a 16/20 h.p. four cylinder, 24/30 h.p. six cylinder and 50 h.p. six cylinder model. The 16/20 h.p. model was to be made available in three wheelbases, 9'-9", 10'-3" or 11'-9" and this was expected to be the most popular model in the range with a predicted 4,000 to be sold, fitted with a S.U. carburettor made under licence at the Adderley Park works. Royalties were paid to the S.U. company, but records of the early payments are no longer available. However, some records from 1920 onwards reveal that royalties totalling £56-8s-9d were paid in 1920, £30-10s-11d in 1921 and £5-13s-0d in 1922. The diminishing payments are probably explained by the ability of the S.U. company to maintain improved supplies of their carburettors, rather than Wolseley making them.

"STELLITE" MOTOR CAR AND THE ELECTRIC & ORDNANCE ACCESSORIES COMPANY LIMITED

Unexpectedly, the company announced plans to re-enter the small car sector of the market with a new 'Voiturette', which some considered to be more of a cycle-car class of vehicle. This was a completely new motor car powered by a four cylinder engine with a bore of 62mm diameter and stroke of 80 mm giving it a capacity of 1,076 c.c. and fitted with a SU type carburettor. With a wheelbase of 8'-0" and track of 3'-10" the car had an overall length of 10'-4", overall width of 4'-8" and the rack and pinion steering gave the car a turning circle of 32'—6". Suspension was by leading quarter elliptic cantilever springs at the front with a tubular front axle and trailing quarter elliptic cantilever springs at the rear with a worm driven rear axle incorporating a two speed gearbox. Initially, the car was being offered as a two seater at £157-10s-0d, but with a three seater model planned for later, the third seat, it is believed, being a "Dickey" seat to the rear of the main body. Tooling up for the first batch of 1,000 cars had already begun with deliveries expected in the early months of 1914. Interestingly, just like the previous Wolseley 'Voiturette', the car was not to be built at Adderley Park, but at the Vickers subsidiary company, Electric & Ordnance Accessories Co.Ltd., in Aston, Birmingham, and the car was not even to be called a Wolseley, but known simply as the "Stellite", derived from the name of the factory in which it was to be built! The "Stellite Works" had been known by that name since at least 1897 when it was occupied by a firm called R.H.Hall Ltd., who made cycles, cycle parts, tools, and electrical equipment under the "Stellite" trade name. The owner of the company sold the business in February 1899 to a Mr Atherton for £55,000, and Mr Hall was retained as manager at a salary of £1,000 per annum, and the company was renamed, The British Electric Works Co.Ltd. In April 1900 the company was sold again, this time to Vickers for £142,000, who, shortly after taking over the company, renamed it the Electric & Ordnance Accessories Company Limited. By 1902 the company employed 900 workers in 14 workshops covering some 68,000 sq.ft., equipped with over 700 machine tools and were then making electric motors, generators, switchboards, meters, fans, telephones and complete sets of railway carriage lighting equipment. The latter equipment included a belt driven dynamo weighing 3.25 cwts, and mounted beneath the carriage, heavy duty dynamo regulator weighing 75 lbs and storage batteries weighing a total of 6 cwts. As well as electrical equipment the company also made "Maxim" and "Pom-Pom" projectiles and cartridge cases up to 18 pounds in Cheston Road, Aston and in a second factory located in Weaman Street close to the city centre. In addition to this serious equipment they were also making Boer War souvenirs in the form of a one pounder "Pom-Pom" shell made into a paper weight or ink pot.

As well as electrical equipment and munitions the company became increasingly involved with the manufacture of motor car components, announcing in November 1907 that they had started to produce the Warner Autometer which was to be sold through Wolseley. In the same year production of universal joints

ILLUSTRATION

Advertisement from 1899 showing a "Stellite" cycle made by The British Electric Works Co. Ltd., in the "Stellite Works", Cheston Road, Aston. The name of the company existed for just over one year, before being changed to the Electric & Ordnance Accessories Co.Ltd.

PHOTOGRAPH

A picture of one of the original "Stellite" motor cars, designed by Wolseley, but built in the "Stellite Works" of the Electric & Ordnance Accessories Co.Ltd. It sold well, and cost £157-10s-0d. After being withdrawn from production during the war, it was re-introduced in March 1919 at the Drews Lane works, still with its Ash chassis frame, but with the rear trans-axle now incorporating a 3 speed gearbox. The car was 4ft 8ins wide, 10ft 9ins long and in 2 seater form cost £285, which was considerably cheaper than the Wolseley 'Ten' with its overhead camshaft engine.

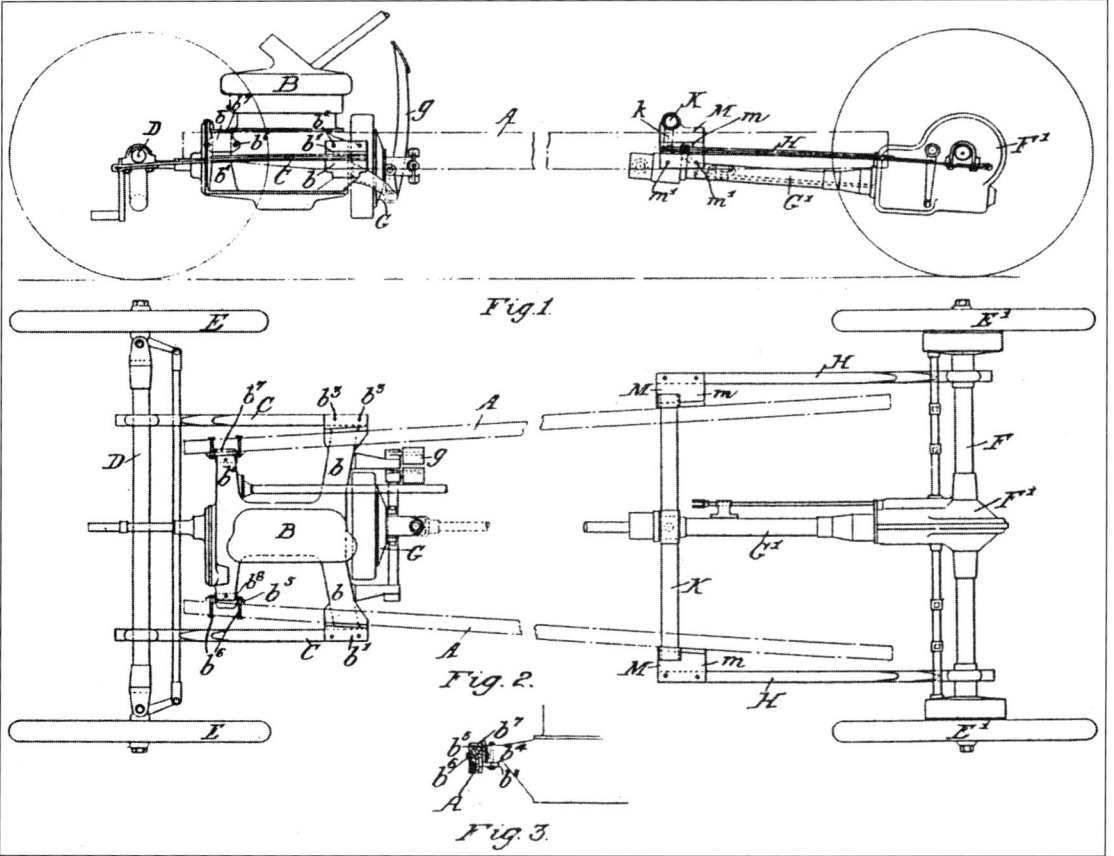

Fig.1

Fig.2.

Fig.3.

Drawing taken from patent number 18685 taken out jointly by Arthur McCormack, Managing Director, and Alfred Remington, the Chief Engineer, on 18th August 1913. This patent covers the design of the "Stellite" car and shows how the car could be built using two sub-frames, the front section to house the front axle, suspension and engine complete with clutch, and the rear section to house the rear suspension and rear axle which was of the transaxle type with a two speed gearbox built into it. This design also allowed cars of differing lengths to be built quite simply by increasing the length of the wooden chassis sidemembers. One of the original "Stellite" cars, built in Aston, was tested at Brooklands at speeds up to 78 m.p.h. and endurance tested for several hours at 60 m.p.h. giving the company such confidence in this little car to consider it 'unbreakable'.

PHOTOGRAPHS

LEFT: A car on the East Works test hill built into the test track to try out the brakes and hill restarting of Wolseley cars. The building in the background was building 'a' erected in 1905 as the Upholstering & Paint Shop.

BELOW: The test hill can also be seen in this picture of the 3 storey "Dustless" Paint Shop completed in 1914, the photograph being taken looking towards Bordesley Green Road from the roadway immediately in front of the 1905 Upholstering & Paint Shop. In later years this buiding housed the wood mill, trimming shop and the apprentice training school for a few years in Morris Commercial days. By 1931 Morris Commercial had erected a building which totally enclosed the open area shown here, which became part of their body building facility and main chassis assembly area after the Second World War.

commenced, and in 1910 the Hall Dual Ignition System was also put into production. In February 1913 the company exhibited at the Heavy Motor Exhibition in Manchester where their range of automotive products included road wheels, front axles, worm drive and bevel drive rear axles, and Timken roller bearings.

At the beginning of the First World War Vickers had bought a site in the Ward End area of Birmingham, covering over 65 acres, and started to erect purpose built premises for the manufacture of ordnance material, the factory becoming an integral part of the Electric & Ordnance Accessories Co.Ltd. Ward End was still a relatively rural area and the production of live munitions was considered quite safe in this area. In May 1915 a 5 cwt van version of the "Stellite" car was put into production at the Aston works, costing £175. The Works Superintendent of the Electric & Ordnance Accessories Co.Ltd., three factories, Mr Walter Livingstone Topple, was awarded the C.B.E. in June 1918 in recognition of his service during the war.

At Wolseley the works were being expanded further and a 40 feet extension was made to the new Iron Foundry in the Britannia Works in 1913, together with a major redevelopment of the area known as Arden Works where work had begun on the construction of a three storey 'J' shaped building built on the site of the reservoir and private houses. The building had a 150 feet frontage to Arden Road which was 42 feet wide with a 31 feet wide short leg 58 feet long and a 42 feet wide long leg taking it up to the Experimental Shop 186 feet long. A 20 feet wide covered way separated the short leg of the new building from the main works building which housed the Marine Engine Department. In the West Works itself a new Boiler House was built near to the railway cottages and close to the south wall of what had been the Iron Foundry and, almost opposite the new boiler house a small group of buildings were erected for a Smithy and Hardening Stores.

About the same time 188 feet of the 20 feet wide open cartway was enclosed by being roofed over and the Trimming Shop and Paint Shop erected in 1903, towards the front of the main office building, was converted into a Drawing Office and extended by a further 21 feet to make the drawing office 77 feet by 64 feet. On the East Works site a Boiler House 26 feet by 47 feet was built next to

PHOTOGRAPHS

ABOVE AND BELOW: These two pictures taken in 1914 show the external and internal views of the new Iron Foundry, building 'r', built in the "Britannia Works" in 1911, with additions made to the building in 1913. This building was demolished about 1934 to make way for the Morris Commercial West Works Extension which housed machine shops and test facilities for the production of engines and gearboxes.

It is interesting to note that two young men, Arnold Pearce and Percy Pritchard, became friends whilst working together in the foundry and decided, in 1914, to set up their own business making cylinder castings for petrol engines. Their first commission was air cooled cylinder castings for the Birmingham made "Radco" 2½ h.p. motor cycle, and their business, named The Midland Motor Cylinder Co.ltd., went on to become one of the largest casting suppliers to the British motor industry.

RIGHT: A 1914 Wolseley 24/30 h.p. model with a Limousine De-Luxe body.

the Engine House and a huge three storey "Dustless" Paint Shop was built 50 feet by 328 feet, each floor being 12 feet high and connected by an internal lift, which measured 12 feet by 18 feet, and an external staircase. Such were the abrupt changes in ground level of the East Works site that the ground and first floors of this building could both be accessed from roadways. The ground floor was a Priming Shop, the first floor the Finishing Shop and the second floor was the Painting and Varnishing Shop. This shop contained a number of cubicles where bodies could stand for a full 24 hours whilst the final coat of varnish dried, the department having a capacity of 48 bodies per week. Parts of the old East Works paint shop, erected in 1904, were now being used as a Finishing Shop and Window Frame Makers Shop.

A total of 11 patents were taken out in 1913, numbers 1953, 3065, 6117, 7819, 12400, 12930, 18685, 26678, 27568, 27569 and 27702. Again, diverse subjects were covered including valve gear, suspensions and a chassis design. The latter, patent number 18685, deals with the design features of the "Stellite" car outlining the principle whereby the front suspension and engine were mounted on one sub-frame and the rear axle and rear suspension were mounted on another sub-frame, allowing the wheelbase of the chassis to be lengthened or shortened without interfering with the main mechanical components. The original "Stellite" had a wooden chassis frame flitched with steel plates, and it would have been quite easy to offer a longer car simply by using longer parts to form the chassis and fitting an alternative body. (The cylinder head design for the "Stellite" engine had been patented in 1912 under patent number 25009) Patents numbers 27568 and 27702 again deal with rear suspensions of the cantilever spring type and 27702 also details a design where auxiliary quarter elliptic springs, connected to a transverse beam, control roll in a vehicle fitted with conventional semi-elliptic road springs.

PHOTOGRAPHS

LEFT: Taken in 1910 both of these pictures show the York Street showroom of The Wolseley Tool & Motor Car Company Limited, situated in the Westminster district of London. For a time all enquiries about Wolseley products were dealt with through the York Street offices, but it soon became apparent that they could be dealt with more efficiently by the factory itself and this work was then transferred to the Adderley Park works.

Lock-up garages were available here enabling owners without garaging space of their own to park their motor cars in dry and secure premises. The facility even included a battery charging service and an area in which to wash cars before being locked away in individual garage spaces.

BELOW: A 1914 works built 25 seater Charabanc body on a 'CL' type passenger chassis. The chassis had a wheelbase of 13ft 9ins, front track of 5ft 6ins, overall length of 20ft 3ins and overall width of 6ft 11ins. The 4 cylinder engine had a bore of 102mm diameter and stroke of 130mm and was rated at 25.6 h.p. Fitted with a cone clutch and 4 speed gearbox the chassis had a double reduction rear axle, a turning circle of 50 feet, weighed 51 cwts and cost £640 in chassis form.

The car range for the 1914 season was comprised of two 16/20 h.p. models with four cylinder engines having a bore of 90mm diameter and stroke of 121mm, with four speed gearboxes and available with either a 10'-4" or 10'-10" wheelbase chassis; two 24/30 h.p. models with six cylinder engines having a bore of 90mm diameter and stroke of 130mm with four speed gearboxes and available with a 10'-11" or 11'-5" wheelbase chassis and two 30/40 h.p. models powered by six cylinder engines with a bore of 102mm diameter and stroke of 140mm, with three speed gearboxes and available with 11'-7" or 12'-1" wheelbase chassis.

In December 1914 a journalist from "Motor Traction" magazine spent a day with a Glasgow grocer, who operated a 12 cwt Wolseley van, to find out what a typical days work entailed delivering groceries. The van made 27 deliveries and covered 49.5 miles, with an actual running time of 3 hours 14 minutes. Four gallons of petrol, at 1s-9d per gallon, were used, giving a fuel consumption of 12.37 m.p.g. with 1.8 stops per mile.

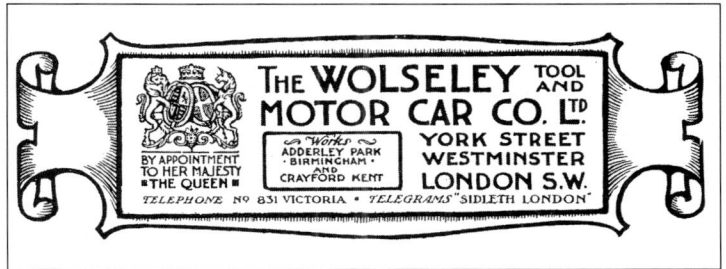

THE **WOLSELEY** TOOL AND **MOTOR CAR CO.** LTD

BY APPOINTMENT TO HER MAJESTY THE QUEEN

Works ADDERLEY PARK · BIRMINGHAM · AND CRAYFORD KENT

YORK STREET WESTMINSTER LONDON S.W.

TELEPHONE No 831 VICTORIA · *TELEGRAMS* "SIDLETH LONDON"

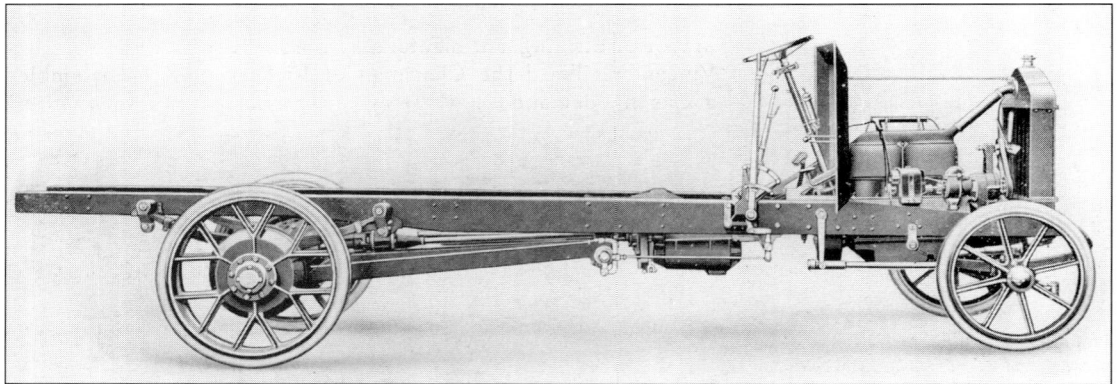

On January 21st a special train from London brought various dignitaries to the Adderley Park works for the ceremonial opening of the latest addition to the factory. Included in the invited guests were, the Rt. Hon. Reginald McKenna Home Secretary, Committee members of the Royal Automobile Club, Chinese, Bulgarian and Roumanian Ministers, representatives of the British Army and Navy and several representatives from various foreign embassies.

The occasion was the opening of the new three storey 'J' shaped building in Arden Road which was to house the production facilities for commercial vehicles and become the centre for the production of marine, aero and other special engines. The basement of this building (the bed of the old reservoir) was to be a store for raw materials, the first floor a general machine shop for commercial vehicle heavy components, the second floor a machine shop for lighter commercial components and the top floor for the sub-assembly of commercial vehicle light components.

A tour of the factory included a visit to the new three storey 'dust-free' Paint Shop on the East Works site and a glimpse into the Experimental Shop where a new paraffin powered marine engine was being developed for British Admiralty Motor Patrol Boats. At a luncheon attended by over 1,000 visitors, including the Lord Mayor of Birmingham Lieutentant Colonel Ernest Martineau, Sir Vincent Cailliard the Chairman of Vickers told the assembled guests that demand for Wolseley motor cars had been so great that the machine shop had been working day and night shifts for the past five years and that production at the factory had risen from 323 cars in 1901 to 692 in 1906, just under 1,300 in 1911 and over 3,000 in 1913. He also announced that the company planned to build 2,000 four cylinder cars, 1,000 six cylinder cars and 1,500 'Stellite' cars during 1914, but events later in the year probably reduced these numbers considerably.

Commercial vehicles in the Wolseley range of vehicles now included the 12 cwt 'CA' type up to the 5 ton 'HR' type. The power units for the commercials were all of four cylinder configuration with capacities of 2.37 litres, 3.08 litres, 4.25 litres, 5.6 litres and the massive 6.58 litre unit used in the 5 tonner. All but the little 12 cwt model were fitted with solid tyres and all featured four speed gearboxes and underslung worm drive rear axles, with chassis prices of £335 12 cwt, £415 1 tonner, £475 30 cwt, £640 for the 'CL' type passenger model, £695 4 tonner, £725 for the 'CR' type Subsidy 3 tonner and £750 for the 5 tonner. The Subsidy type 3 tonner would be built in large numbers during the First World War and some of the heavier lorry chassis would be used as the basis for cumbersome looking armoured cars and even some of the car chassis would still be built during the war as the basis for ambulances.

Strangely, although the company had manufactured petrol electric commercial vehicles of its own design in the past, it was now the sole British concessionaire for the American Baker electric commercial vehicles, a range from about 10 cwts up to 5 tons. Three 3½ ton Baker flatbed lorries were supplied to the Vickers factory at Dartford where they were used to transport material between Dartford and Woolwich Arsenal and in Birmingham the Dunlop Rubber Company operated a 3½ ton Baker van. These vehicles had

PHOTOGRAPHS

TOP: The "Arden Works" built in 1913 to house production facilities for commercial vehicles and marine engines, viewed from Arden Road, looking towards the crossroads with Bordesley Green Road. In 1914 a three storey building was erected where the wall is seen here, the new building being primarily for the assembly of aero engines, an activity which soon spread to the upper floors of the new "Arden Works" building. In fact, these two buildings would be connected by a landing built to bridge the gap between their top floors.

The two lower photographs show the Class 'A' three ton Subsidy Type lorry in chassis form, and as a complete vehicle. Based on the 'CR' type 13ft 9ins wheelbase chassis the vehicle was powered by a 4 cylinder side valve engine rated at 34.2 h.p., with a bore of 117mm diameter, and stroke of 130mm. The front track was 5ft 6ins and overall dimensions were, 7ft wide, 21ft long and with a 53ft turning circle. Fitted with a cone type clutch, four speed gearbox and double reduction rear axle, the vehicle in chassis form weighed 3 tons and cost £725.

a working range of 35 to 40 miles between battery charges and cost £605 for a 1 tonner, £729 for a 2 tonner and £939 for a 3½ tonner, all in chassis form. The use of battery electric vehicles in Britain increased sharply after the First World War and several new companies were set up in Britain for their manufacture, many of American origin. The Baker company itself appears to have gone out of business in 1916 and Wolseley, unfortunately, discontinued its own range of commercial vehicles at the end of the war, but may well have found a niche in the market had they introduced a battery electric truck of their own design into the post war market place.

In April 1914 a two storey office was built in the West Works on a site previously occupied by some of the single storey workshops which had their frontage onto the open cartway which ran north - south through the works. The building was 170 feet long by 22 feet wide, the ground floor being 16 feet high and the first floor 12 feet high, the overall height being 37 feet 6 inches. The ground floor housed general offices and the first floor the Works Engineers Office and the M.T. Drawing Office. In the Britannia Works one of the old railway carriage construction buildings was demolished and a three storey building constructed measuring 50 feet by 260 feet and with a bridge connecting the first floor Aero Engine Erecting Shop to the 'J' shaped building erected in 1913 in the Arden Works. The two upper floors, 17 feet high and 15 feet high respectively, were connected via an internal lift and external staircase. The ground floor, although 13 feet high was, for almost three quarters of its length, below pavement level to Arden Road and was designated as a Timber Stores.

The company changed its name to Wolseley Motors Limited in July and war was declared with Germany on 4th August. Such were the austerity measures of war that the company letterheads were simply overprinted in red ink with the new name until after hostilities had ceased in 1919. Also in July, the company made an issue of £500,000 5% First Mortgage Debenture Stock and the parent company Vickers announced that the Wolseley company had made a profit of £90,940 in 1911, £121,300 in 1912 and £162,968 in 1913 and that the company's assets were valued at £1,196,348. This makes an interesting comparison to the profits of the Austin Motor Company Ltd., of £39,174 in 1911, £55,745 in 1912 and £41,129 in 1913. With the outbreak of war the company switched its resources to the production of commercial vehicles, ambulances and other military equipment. A 24/30 h.p. truck with canvas tilt bodywork and wire wheels with twin wheels on the rear axle was supplied to the Royal Navy Aeroplane Section for carrying ammunition and six 24/30 h.p. ambulances were built for the American Women's Relief Committee in London as their donation to the war effort.

However, patents were still being taken out although the number had reduced dramatically to just eight. These were numbers 99, 3269, 13631, 13640, 15311, 18781, 21695 and 22706 and dealt with motor car hoods, gearboxes, wheels, tyres and suspension.

Despite the war the company was still able to offer motor cars for the 1915 season, albeit with a reduced range of just three basic models, but still with a wide option of bodies. The three basic models being offered at this time were the 16/20 h.p., 24/30 h.p. and 30/40 h.p. chassis, all being fitted with 4 speed gearboxes, and the larger two models both featuring 6 cylinder engines.

The 16/20 h.p. model was available in two wheelbases, 10ft 4ins and 11ft 1in, both chassis having sidemembers which were flat, excepting a slight upward sweep over the rear axle. Suspension was by semi-elliptic leaf springs at the front, with underslung semi-elliptics to the rear axle on short wheelbase models, and by the company's patented cantilever suspension to the rear axle on long wheelbase models. The latter consisted of very long inverted semi-elliptic springs fixed at the springs centres to abutments on the sides of the chassis sidemembers, with their front ends shackled to the chassis frame, and cantilevered rear ends fixed to the rear axle casings. The 4 cylinder 16/20 h.p. engine had a bore of 90mm diameter, stroke of 121mm, capacity of 3.07 litres and RAC rating of 20.3 h.p. A fabric faced cone clutch transmitted power to the gearbox via a short open propshaft, then by a longer open propshaft to the underslung worm drive rear axle with a ratio of 4.1:1.

Bodies available for the 16/20 h.p. chassis included a Touring Car for the short wheelbase model at £435, with the rest of the bodies suitable for long wheelbase chassis only. These included a Torpedo Phaeton at £520, Coupe Landaulette at £575, Flush Sided Landaulette at £665, Cabrio Phaeton at £625, Flush Sided Limousine at £665, Cabriolet at £705, and a 2 seater at £500.

The 24/30 h.p. chassis had a wheelbase of 11ft 5ins, the chassis sidemembers being swept downwards to the rear of the drivers seat, to improve access into the rear passenger compartment, before being swept upwards over the rear axle. Suspension on both 6 cylinder powered chassis was by semi-elliptic leaf springs at the front and patented cantilevered springs to the rear.

The engine had a bore of 90mm diameter, stroke of 130mm, capacity of 4.96 litres and RAC rating of 30.4 h.p. Ignition was by H.T. magneto with variable timing from a hand control, and an electric starter was standard equipment. A multi-plate, metal to metal, clutch running in oil, transmitted power by a short propshaft to the gearbox, then by open propshaft to the bevel drive rear axle which had a ratio of 3.6:1. The braking system consisted of a foot pedal operated strap brake acting on a gearbox mounted drum, and expanding brake shoes inside drums at the rear wheels, operated by a hand lever.

Bodies for the 24/30 h.p. chassis included a Torpedo Phaeton at £745, Flush Sided Phaeton at £880, Flush Sided Limousine at £880, Cabrio-Phaeton at £845, and a Cabriolet at £930.

The largest wartime model still available, albeit for a very limited period, the 30/40 h.p. 6 cylinder chassis had a wheelbase of 12ft 4ins. The engine had a bore of 102mm diameter, stroke of 140mm and RAC rating of 38.4 h.p. A dual ignition system was fitted comprising H.T. magneto and induction coil, and an electric starter was standard.

Transmission and braking system followed the specification of the 24/30 h.p. model, although the larger model had a rear axle ratio of 3.2:1. All chassis featured petrol tanks mounted transversely across the rear of the chassis frames, the tanks being shaped to fit the curvature of the underside of the chassis sidemembers.

The choice of bodies for the top of the range model was even more restricted than those of the smaller chassis, reflecting that the body building facilities at the works were being increasingly pressed into the manufacture of ambulances, military vehicle bodies, and aeroplane propellers. However, the bodies available for the

PHOTOGRAPHS

Even after the start of the First World War the company was still able to offer a car such as this 1915 Flush Sided Landaulette, based upon the 30/40 h.p. chassis shown below. Powered by a 6 cylinder engine with a capacity of 6.86 litres this luxury 4 to 6 seater had C.A.V. electric lighting, electric starter as standard equipment, and cost £1,130 ready for the road, and delivered to any railway station in the United Kingdom

The chassis photograph illustrates the clean and uncluttered arrangement of the basic chassis design, and shows the 6 cylinder engine made up from 3 paired cylinder blocks, the patented rear cantilevered suspension, and the petrol tank mounted transversely across the rear of the chassis frame, which on earlier models had been mounted longitudinally inside the chassis frame.

30/40 h.p. chassis included a Torpedo Phaeton at £995, Flush Sided Landaulette at £1,130, Flush Sided Limousine at £1,130 and a Cabriolet at £1,180.

Customers could still order optional equipment, at extra cost, like a Warner Autometer speedometer at £11 including fitting; waterproof canvas seat covers for open cars at £10-10s-0d; leather valances to fit between the body and running boards to cover the chassis frame at £4-4s-0d, polished wood cabinets at £4; tool cabinets mounted on the running board, either polished or painted in the body colour, at £5, leather pockets in the backs of the front seats at £3-3s-0d, and Morocco upholstery available in Limousine and Landaulette bodies for an additional £5. An electric starter was available for the 16/20 h.p. model at an extra £18, as was dual ignition at £6, and the standard nickel finish of the chassis could be changed to brass plating for £5.

Adderley Park Works

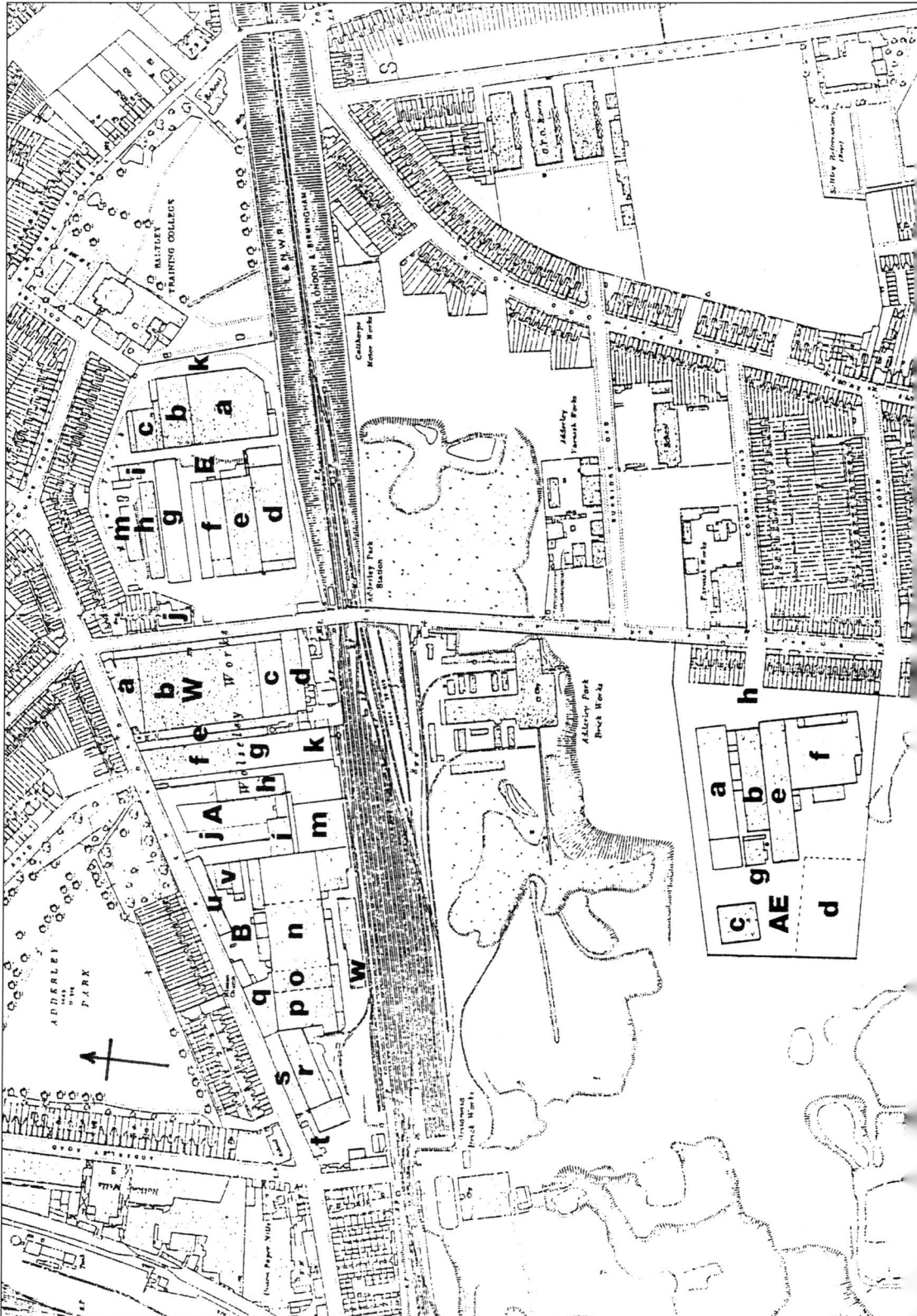

Wolseley

AERO SITE (AE)

a. Woodworking & Assembly Shop.
b. Sawmill.
c. Timber Store.
d. Military Enclosure.
e. Erecting & Viewing Shop.
f. Automatic Machine Shop.
g. Boiler House.
h. Main Entrance to site.

EAST WORKS (E)

a. Window Frame Makers, Finishing Shop and Varnishing Shop.
b. Upholstering Shop.
c. Body Mounting Shop.
d. Car Finished Test Shop.
e. Shell Shop.
f. Shell Shop Extensions.
g. Paint Shop.
h. Body Stores.
i. Engine House & Boiler House.
j. Two storey Mess Rooms.
k. Car Test Track around perimeter of site.
m. Wing Shop.

WEST WORKS (W)

a. Drawing Office over Rough Stores.
b. Machine Shops.(including c & d).
e. Single storey Workshops, plus two storey Works Engineers Office and M.T. Drawing Office.
f. Engine Assembly Shop.
g. Forging & Smiths Shop.
k. Assembly Shop.

ARDEN WORKS (A)

h. Plating Shop.
i. Experimental Shop.
j. Three storey building housing Machine Shops, Assembly Shops and Engine Assembly. Built over site of old reservoir.

BRITANNIA WORKS (B)

m. Chassis Erecting Shop.
n. Sawmills & Body Shop.
o. Carriage Smiths.
p. Aluminium Foundry.
q. Repair Shops.
r. Iron Foundry.
s. Repair Shop.
t. Offices.
u. Three storey building housing Timber Store and Aero Engine Assembly Shop.
v. Engine Test Houses.
w. Chassis Frame Construction Shop.

AERO SITE - BORDESLEY GREEN

In January 1915 the company acquired a 7.78 acres site in Bordesley Green Road, about 250 yards south of the Adderley Park Works, to build a new factory specifically for the production of aircraft. With no idea of how long hostilities would last this was a major decision by the company to expand into this new field of warfare, but their foresight was to pay off and hundreds of S.E.5a fighter planes were to be built and put into active service from this new factory.

The first building on the site was a single storey Construction Shed, 300 feet long by 84 feet wide and designed to give a clear centre span 45 feet wide by 17 feet high and with an overall height of 26 feet. The Construction Shed, which was steel framed and clad with steel sheeting, was soon joined by a Timber Store 150 feet long by 30 feet wide, of similar construction, and built 10 feet away from the Construction Shed. In March 1915 toilet facilities and a Heating Chamber were added to the south side of the Construction Shed and in July another Timber Store, 100 feet by 100 feet, was built 174 feet north of the Construction Shed. At about the same time the original Timber Store was extended by 40 feet and the building converted into a Sawmill. The 10 feet wide gap between this building and the Construction Shed was then roofed over to provide a Drawing Office, Staff Mess Room, Girls Mess Room and Mens Mess Room.

In 1916 a massive expansion of the Aero Site took place when the Construction Shed was extended by 80 feet and became the Woodworking and Assembly Shop and the Sawmill was doubled in width, to 60 feet, and the length increased to 292 feet. Expansion was so rapid that buildings were being modified almost as soon as they were erected.

Alongside the enlarged Sawmill a new single storey Erecting and Viewing Shop was built 70 feet wide by 380 feet long and standing 40 feet high to the top of its centrally mounted roof ventilators. However, the most prominent development on the site was the erection of a single storey Automatic Machine Shop, 200 feet by 200 feet which, with its own two storey offices at the front of the building, for administration, helped to make the Aero Site almost self sufficient.

Seven patents were taken out in 1915, numbers 4172, 4303, 6142, 7557, 8296, 16306 and 17944. Number 4172 dealt with the propulsion of ships powered by internal combustion engines and electric motors, number 6142 with improvements to ambulance bodies and number 17944 with lockable rear axle differentials. This was of particular interest as vehicles being operated in appalling battlefield conditions would benefit from such devices where the ability to provide extra traction could be the difference between life or death.

In 1917 an Oil Separating Plant, 20 feet by 40 feet, was added to the north side of the Automatic Machine Shop and the site was increased to 12.57 acres following the acquisition of land along its south border. The first building to be built on the new extension was a Temporary Canteen, 112 feet long by 34 feet 6 inches wide, with a Kitchen, Stores and seating area for 288 people, giving some indication of the size of the workforce employed at the Aero Site. (Although all the buildings had been granted only Temporary Licenses "for the duration of the war", most were still standing as late as 1937.)

In January 1915 the Iron Foundry in the Britannia Works was extended by a further 45 feet, but in the East Works major changes were being implemented to cater for the ever increasing war work. Part of the Mill which was being used as the Driving School and Stores was converted into a Shell Shop and in April this was enlarged by the erection of a temporary single storey building 50 feet wide by 260 feet long, being 15 feet 9 inches high to the eaves and 25 feet high overall. A 48 feet section of this building was converted to Girls Mess Room and Toilet, complete with Matrons Room in June, showing the ever increasing need to employ women in heavy industry during these trying times. A further extension was made to the Shell Shop in the same month when another single storey temporary building was erected alongside the first extension, measuring 33 feet wide by 260 feet long. The Boiler House built onto the Engine House was also enlarged in 1915 by adding a building 14 feet wide by 56 feet long.

Some Wolseley commercial vehicles were still being produced for the civilian market, for such people as Waring & Gillow Ltd., Sheffield Corporation and W & R Jacob & Co.Ltd. Even the Electric & Ordnance Accessories company built some commercial vehicles at this time, namely a 5 cwt van version of the "Stellite" small car priced at £175.

Since December 1914 over 1,000 machine tools had been installed and put into operation in the Shell Shop alone, so great was the driving force behind the war effort. Lloyd George, the Chancellor of the Exchequer, in a speech made on 28th February, highlighted the importance of the engineering industry when he said, "This is an engineers war and it will be won or lost owing to the efforts or shortcomings of engineers. Output is everything in this war."

On Friday 23rd July 1915 His Majesty King George visited the Adderley Park Works to observe at first hand the amount of war work being undertaken by the company. The visit lasted only 45 minutes, but the King had also visited the B.S.A. works in Small Heath on the same day. The Wolseley Works Band, together with a section of Number 1 Supernumerary Company of the 6th Warwickshire Regiment accompanied the King from the Britannia Works in Arden Road to the Main Office entrance where he was met by Mr. Ernest Hopwood and Mr. A. McCormack, Joint Managing Directors(Mr McCormack was also a Director of Vickers Ltd) and Mr. B.L.P Caillard Resident Director. The King was also introduced to Mr. A.Jacob-Secretary, Mr. A.A. Remington - Chief Engineer and Mr. Max R. Lawrence - Superintendent of the Heavy Vehicle, Marine & Aero Sections. (Mr Lawrence appears to have had several jobs, as he had been Works Manager until December 1912 when he was reported to have left the company to take up the position of Lancashire Area Representative for Messrs J & E Hall Ltd., who sold Halford spares. However, in October 1912 he was again reported as having resigned from the Wolseley factory to manage the Wolseley depot at Deansgate, Manchester. Prior to working at Adderley Park he had been Works Manager for the Lanchester Motor Company in Montgomery Street, Birmingham, an appointment he took up in January 1901 at the princely salary of £3 per week) After being taken to the Reception Room to sign the

PHOTOGRAPHS

TOP: On Friday 23rd July 1915 King George visited the Adderley Park works to observe at first hand the war work being undertaken by the company. This Reception Room situated to the right hand side of the main office entrance in West Works was where the King signed the visitors book before being escorted on a tour of the works. In later years this room became the waiting room for visitors to the Morris Commercial company when they took over the Adderley Park works in 1929.

BOTTOM: The King leaving the East Works through the lower of two ornate gateways which accessed the site. A large group of workers are seen standing out in the rain after the King had toured the Shell Shop which was situated in the building with the two arched doorways to the right upper corner of this picture. The building made from sheets of material to the left upper corner was one of the temporary Shell Shop extension built some months earlier.

The visit had been preceded by a violent storm which had flooded the works railway siding and part of Arden Road, but most of the rainwater had been cleared away by Wolseley workers before the arrival of the Royal Train, although, as this picture indicates the rain still persisted during the Royal visit.

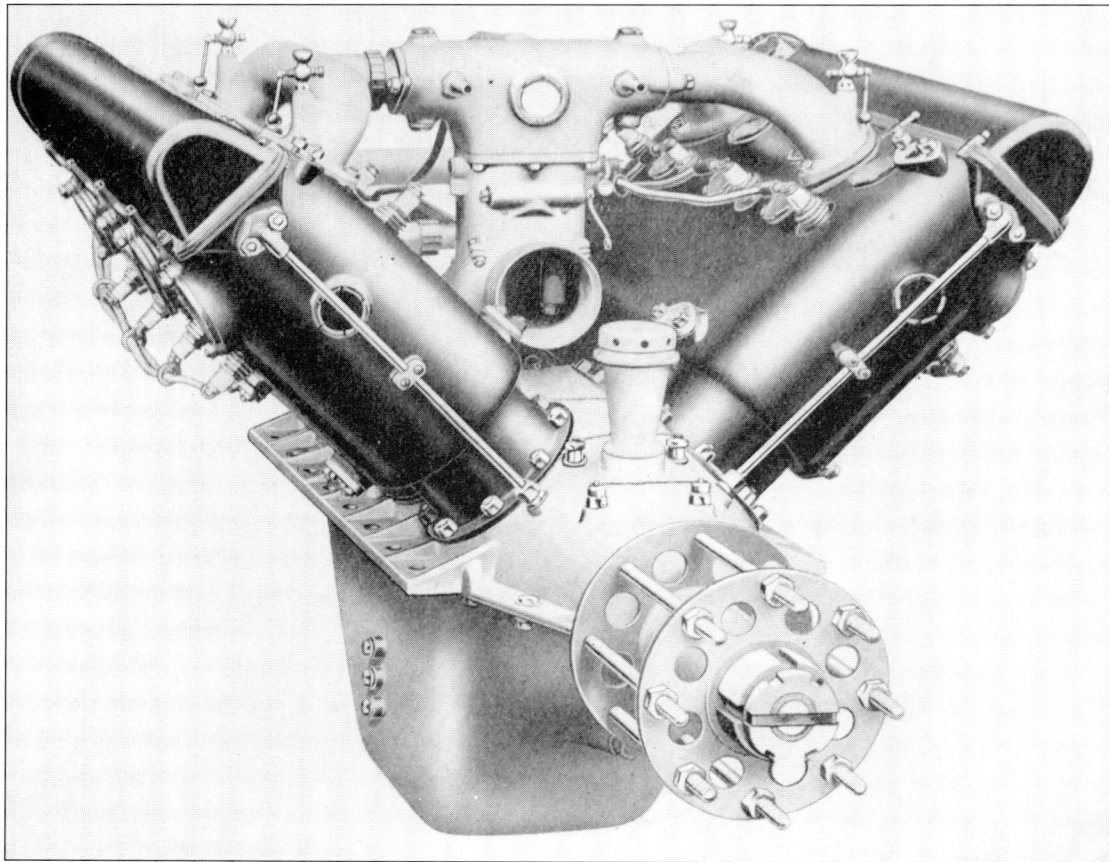

TOP: The Wolseley "Python" V8 aero engine showing the propeller drive on the crankshaft and the massive air intake to the carburettor mounted between the banks of cylinders. The engine had a bore of 120mm diameter and stroke of 130mm, compression ratio of 5.3:1, developed 180 b.h.p. at 1,800 r.p.m., had a specific fuel consumption of 0.59 pints/bhp hr and consumed lubricating oil at the rate of 7 to 9 pints per hour. The overall dimensions were 59" long, 33" wide, 32" high and had a dry weight of 465 lbs.

BELOW: A general view of the aircraft engine test houses located in the Britannia Works. The building in the background is part of the 3 storey 'J' shaped building erected in the Arden Works. The water cooled engines were tested using reaction torque stands activated by the thrust of the propellers, some of which can be seen here outside each test house. The front and sides of the test houses were covered by heavy torpedo netting. All the engines shown here were of the 'geared' type where the propeller drive was geared vertically from the engine crankshaft to allow a Lewis gun to be fired through the hollow drive shaft.

ILLUSTRATION

Illustration from Patent Number 18168 taken out in 1912 by Arthur McCormack for an air cooled aero engine with water cooled exhaust valves. Apparently air cooled aero engines of this period suffered from exhaust valve siezure caused by localised overheating and this design eliminated this problem. In 1914 the company built V8 engines to this design with a bore of 102mm diameter and stroke of 140mm giving a capacity of 9.15 litres.

vistors book the King was escorted across Bordesley Green Road to the East Works entrance. Upon entering the factory His Majesty toured the Shell Shop and spoke individually to a small group of wounded soldiers brought to the works for the occasion from the hospital at Bournbrook, Birmingham.

By this time the company employed some 5,000 people and the Vickers company as a whole employed another 6,000 in its various Birmingham factories.

After a quick tour of the West Works Machine Shops, where he was introduced to Mr. Barnsley, Mr. Royce and Mr. Wattis, the King visited the Aero Engine Assembly Shop where he was introduced to Mr. Pitt, Mr. Abraham, Mr. Prestage and Mr. Oak. In the Heavy Vehicle Erecting Shop Mr. Leeding, Mr. Dougill and Mr. Haddleton were presented to the King and, after visiting the Coachsmiths Shop and Aluminium Foundry in the Britannia Works, where a small selection of aluminium castings been put on display, His Majesty boarded the Royal Train standing in the works siding alongside the Chassis Construction Shop.

This was a time of great national patriotism and it was not unknown for men not serving in His Majesty's Services to be given a white feather if people thought they were evading their responsibility to King and Country and members of the armed forces were also known to be out on the streets checking out men who should be in the forces.. The Wolseley company issued their employees with a Workers Certificate measuring about 5"x3", possibly to avoid the embarrassment of being challenged on the streets, which read, "This is to Certify that the Bearer........is in the employ of Wolseley Motors Ltd.,of Adderley Park, Birmingham, and that his services are required by this firm in order to enable them to carry out Fully and Promptly the requirements of the British Government for the supply of War Material. For Wolseley Motors Ltd.", and signed by Alec McCormack, Director.

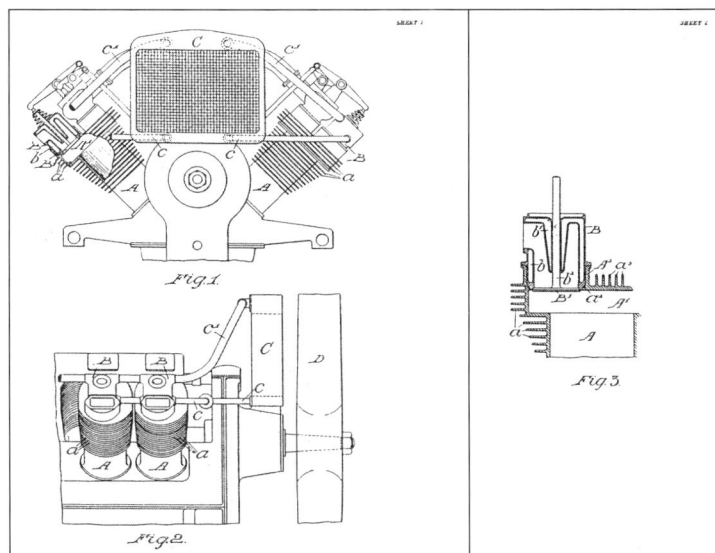

LEFT-TOP: A 'WB' type 70 h.p. Wolseley-Renault aero engine which produced 76 b.h.p. at 1,800 r.p.m., weighed 440 lbs and had a specific fuel consumption of .76 pints/bhp-hr. and consumed lubricating oil at the rate of 6½ pints/hr. This engine, like the 'WC' and 'WX' types had its cylinders offset to those of the opposite bank allowing conventional con-rods to be used, but on the 80 h.p. 'WS' type the cylinders were directly opposite each other making it necessary to use a main con-rod and hinged con-rod to each big end bearing. Carburation was via the Claudel Hobson carburettor seen here mounted at the end of the extended inlet pipes to the far right of the picture.

BOTTOM: One of the air cooled Wolseley-Renault aero engines coupled up to a Heenan & Froude water dynamometer for performance testing. The top section of the air ducting has been removed to allow free circulation of air from the overhead duct which supplied cold air during testing. The engines would have been belt driven from an overhead layshaft for two hours 'running-in', after which the oil would have been changed before the engine was started up under its own power for a 3 hours test programme. After successfully completing this test programme the engine would be completely stripped, examined, and if found to be satisfactory, re-assembled and tested for a further 30 minutes on full load before being passed off.

BELOW: A view inside one of the aero engine erecting shops located in building 'u' in the "Britannia Works", with lines of completed Wolseley-Renault air cooled engines assembled tested and ready for despatch to the Aero Site and to other aircraft construction works around the country.

Aero engines had been produced by the company for some years and were becoming increasingly more important as aircraft were now being used for warfare. A range of four Renault designed Wolseley-Renault air cooled aero engines was put into production, the four different models being, the types 'WB' and 'WC' rated at 70 h.p., the type 'WX' at 75 h.p. and type 'WS' at 80 h.p. These had bore/stroke dimensions of 96mm diameter by 120mm for 'WB' and 'WC' (6.95litres), 100mm diameter by 120mm for type 'WX' (7.54 litres) and 105mm diameter by 130mm for the largest type 'WS' engine of 9.0 litres. The valve design was exhaust over inlet operated by a single camshaft located between the banks of cylinders which were each clamped to the crankcase by four bolts, the clamp, in the shape of an 'X' spanning the cylinder heads which were cast separately to the cylinders. The aluminium crankcase was cast in teo parts with the dividing line at the crankshaft centre line, the upper part containing the crankshaft bearings and camshaft, the lower part formed the oil sump. These engines were used in the de Havilland designed B.E.2c reconnaissance/fighter built at the Aero Site. This was one of the first aircraft to have a full set of engineering drawings which allowed construction of the aircraft to be contracted out to various companies around Britain allowing increased output to be achieved without overloading the aircraft factories themselves which were not only trying to do production runs, but were also engaged in the design and development of improved forms of fighters and bombers. Some 2,000,000 drawings were issued to manufacturers building the B.E.2c, which cost £1,072-10s-0d for the airframe, less the engine, instruments and equipment, plus £522-10s-0d for the engine. The wing assemblies became a standard design for other aircraft and were even used as the outer wings of the R.A.F.4a. This must have been the first serious attempt to mass produce an aircraft and Mr. J.D.Pitt of Wolseley, was made a member of the Aero Engine Committee of the Society of British Aircraft Constructors, and for his contribution to the Air Board at this time, Alfred Remington was to be awarded the O.B.E.

LEFT-TOP: (BMIHT photos) Although badly damaged this picture illustrates an important period in the company's history about 1915 - 1916. The aircraft is a de Havilland designed B.E.2c reconnaissance/fighter developed by Farnborough from the original B.E.1 type. With a wingspan of 37 feet the plane was powered by a Renault designed V8 ducted, air cooled engine with the exhaust pipes positioned vertically in front of the forward cockpit which housed the observer. The straps on the starboard side of the aircraft were used to hold a vertical conical box camera and the pilot had to change photographic plates after taking each picture whilst piloting the aircraft and avoiding enemy aircraft! The plane could carry about 160 lbs of bombs and equipment and is shown here in the Military Enclosure 'AE' 'e' to the rear of the Aero Site in Bordesley Green Road. The building with the curved roof was the Sawmill and the other building to the left was the Erecting & Viewing Shop.

BOTTOM: Although untidy in appearance this was the main airframe construction shop where B.E.2c frames can be seen during assembly. The lower frame members were of timber, the rest of the frame being of metal tubes and tensioned steel wires. Towards the centre of the shop and just to the left of the fly-press stands an air cooled V8 engine with vertical exhaust outlets and just visible in the far left corner is a V12 Wolseley-Renault air cooled engine, which was also manufactured by the company.

BELOW: The Covering Room, 'Ae', on the Aero Site which measured 80ft by 42ft and was 26ft high to the ridge. One could hardly believe that this picture was taken in the middle of a war, with the women hand sewing fabric onto aircraft wings and tailplanes.

During the first year of the war 530 aircraft and 141 aero engines had been built in Britain, rising to 7,137 aircraft and 8,917 engines between August 1915 and March 1917, 13,521 aircraft and 13,979 engines from April 1917 to December 1917 and 26,685 aircraft and 29,561 engines from January 1918 to October 1918, a tremendous achievement by and standard.

Some of the other engines developed for fighter planes included Wolseley "Python","Adder" and "Viper" water cooled vee 8's with overhead camshafts, based upon Hispano type 34 and 36 engines. With power outputs of 150 b.h.p to 210 b.h.p. these engines had a capacity of 11.76 litres. The "Adder" engine had the propeller shaft driven through reduction gearing above the crankshaft and, by making the shaft hollow, allowed a Lewis Gun to be mounted between the two banks of cylinders to fire through the hollow propeller shaft. Early examples of the Wolseley built high output "Adder" engine suffered from crankshaft failure, but supplies were so urgently needed that these engines were built into airframes for operational service, but with the engines maximum speed limited to 1,750 r.p.m. to prevent running into the 'critical' speed band where failures occurred. These engines developed full power at 2,000 r.p.m., had a specific fuel consumption of 0.61 pints/bhp-hr and consumed oil at the rate of 10-12 pints per hour. These were used to power the S.E.5a fighters also built at the Aero Site. Wolseley was contracted to build 550 and the Vickers factory at Crayford 1,150. The S.E.5a production machine had a total loaded weight of 1,980 lbs, a maximum speed of 120 m.p.h. at 15,000 feet, maximum ceiling of 19,500 feet and an endurance of 3 hours in the air.

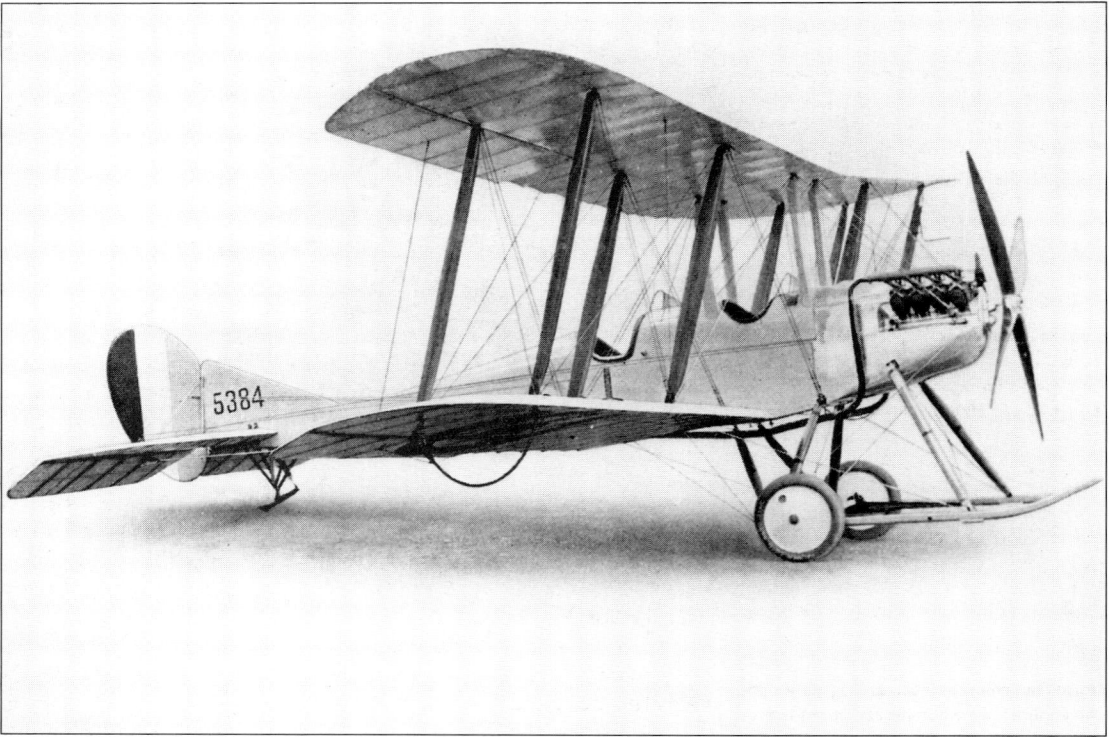

PHOTOGRAPHS

LEFT-TOP: A B.E.2c reconnaissance/fighter plane, probably destined for service with the Royal Naval Air Services as it is fitted with skids forward of the main wheeled undercarriage. The Wolseley-Renault air cooled engine can be seen quite clearly with its exhaust pipes positioned beneath the aircraft. The original B.E.1. type had been powered by a much heavier Wolseley water cooled engine.

BOTTOM: (BMIHT photo) In 1914 part of the East Works Mill number 3 (building 'Ee') was converted into a huge machine shop for the production of shell cases and here we see a predominately young women workers at their machines which stand silent for this specially posed picture. (Even the overhead layshafts show no signs of movement). Although this building had Northern roof lights the general lighting was very poor and the oil marks on the left hand wall, from the flapping leather drive belts, show that conditions in the Shell Shop were far from ideal, but these women are owed a debt of gratitude for their work during the First World War, almost as much as the young men who endured more horrific conditions in the trenches of Flanders.

BELOW: (BMIHT photo) In January 1917 plans were submitted for permission to erect a four storey building, 200 feet long, running parallel to the railway track in the West Works. This picture was taken in that new building in 1918 and shows gun mountings being assembled, probably in the dying days of the war. Only one gun barrel can be seen in the picture, suggesting that complete guns were not assembled at the works, the one barrel being used to ensure correct fitment and alignment when the mountings reached their final assembly point.

The test procedures carried out by Wolseley on their aero engines was extremely thorough and deserves mentioning. A finished engine was mounted on a test rig where it would be belt driven by an electric motor for 2 hours. The engine would then be run under its own power and loading would be gradually increased until the engine was shown to be delivering its designed power output. This would be followed by 3 hours of further 'running-in'. After this initial 5 hours of running the engine would be sent back to the Erecting Shop where it would be stripped completely and all the parts inspected. If everything was still satisfactory the engine would be rebuilt and returned to the test shop for a further half hour of running under its own power. However, had problems arose during the initial test, or during the strip examination, the engine would have been rebuilt and tested for a full hour prior to being despatched from the works. The engine test facilities were by this time located in a group of buildings in the Britannia Works adjacent to the 3 storey 'J' shaped building erected in 1913 for the production of commercial vehicle components. (It is believed that most of Wolseley's early aero engine design work had been carried out by Arthur Rowledge who was Chief Draughtsman with the company until 1914 when he took up an appointment with Napier. Whilst working for Wolseley Rowledge had lived in Dora Road in the Small Heath area of Birmingham. However, Rowledge moved on again in May 1921 to take up an appointment with Rolls-Royce where he designed probably the most famous engine in British aircraft history, the World War 2 "Merlin", a design, sadly, rarely assigned to this brilliant, but retiring, engine designer!)

WOLSELEY MOTORS LIMITED
AERO SITE BLOCK PLAN — 1918

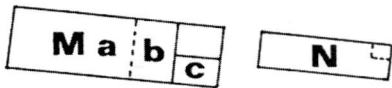

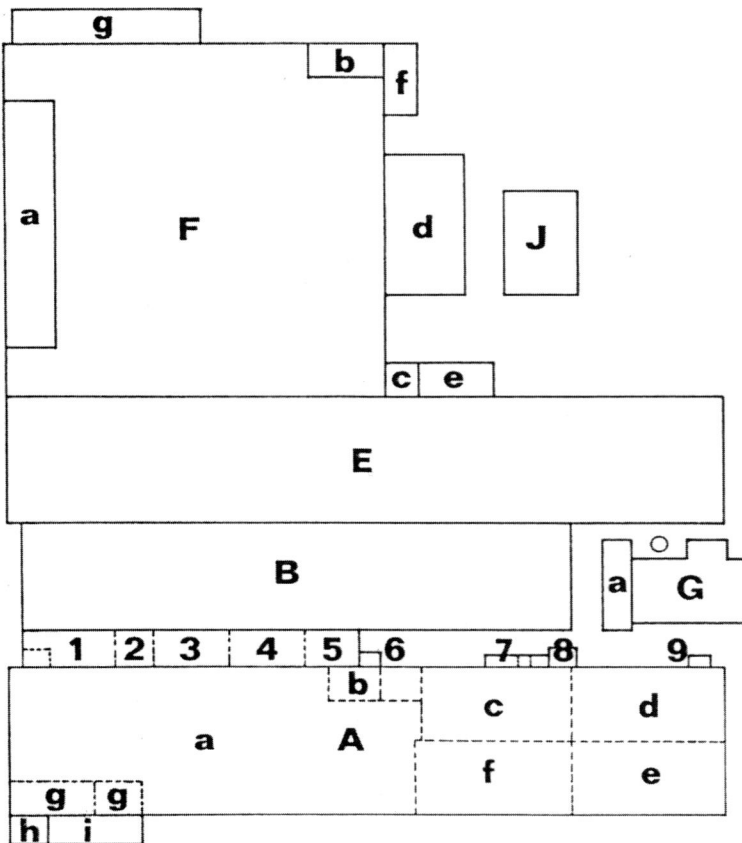

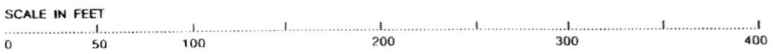

M a b c

N

N

g

b
f

a

F

d

J

c e

E

B

a G

1 2 3 4 5 6   7 8   9

b

a   A   c   d

f   e   C

g g

h i

SCALE IN FEET

0   50   100   200   300   400

NOTE

The company was supplying engines for airships made by Vickers in 1920, which included the R9 powered by four 180 b.h.p. engines, NRP6 powered by two 180 b.h.p. engines, and for the largest Vickers airship then in production, the R80, four 250 b.h.p. engines. The R80 was 525 feet long, 70 feet in diameter, weighed 38 tons, and had a range of 3,900 miles.

Despite the war and the cost of additional plant and machinery the company announced a net profit of £115,012 for 1915. As the war continued so did the expansion of the factory and in May 1916 a Pump House, 13 feet by 30 feet 6 inches was added to the rear of the first Shell Shop extension in East Works and in July the M.T. Drawing Office in the West Works was enlarged by building an extension 17 feet by 60 feet out above the roof of the workshops. Finally, in November 1916 a covered stairway 10 feet 9 inches wide by 49 feet 3 inches long was built to the rear of the Shell Shop and part of the Window Frame Makers Shop had been converted into two mess rooms, a Mens Mess Room 24 feet by 144 feet and a Girls Mess Room 27 feet by 144 feet. In January of the following year a 122 feet length of the open roadway between the Shell Shop and these mess rooms had been roofed over enabling personnel to get to the mess rooms protected from the weather.

A total of 7 patents were applied for in 1916, numbers 104085, 104968, 108242, 108944, 109099, 110045 and 110797, dealing mainly with aircraft engines. Numbers 104968 and 108242 cover the design for triple bank overhead camshaft drives and cylinder block construction for an 18 cylinder water cooled aircraft engine and 109099 shows the design for an aircraft carburettor which automatically weakened the mixture according to altitude.

By now aircraft engines and spares, together with complete aircraft and parts were in full production, together with shells, guns, gun mountings, gun director firing gear and sighting gear (the latter being patented by the company), as well as military lorries, cars, armoured cars and ambulances. When the war ended the company had produced almost 4,000 aero engines, 700 complete aircraft, 850 wing and tail assemblies, 6,000 propellers and more than 1,000 gun mountings and telescopic sights.

In January 1917 the Shell Shop Pump House was extended by 10 feet 4 inches and, although called a pump house, a works drawing would appear to indicate that this building actually housed four giant electric motors to drive the overhead lineshafts in the shell shop. The new extension was to house a 50 h.p. electric motor which ran at 750 r.p.m. and drove a 48 inches diameter lineshaft pulley at 196 r.p.m.

On the West Works site larger extensions were planned and the first of these was a four storey building measuring 42 feet wide by 200 feet long to house Jig, Tool & Gauge Shops, and built parallel to the railway siding. A bridge was built from the third floor of this new building, out above the roofs of the single storey workshops, to join up with the top floor of the 'J' shaped building erected in 1913 in the Arden Works. Standing 78 feet high overall with floor heights of 14 feet 9 inches, 15 feet 6 inches, 16 feet 9 inches and 20 feet 9 inches respectively, this building added 33,600 square feet of capacity to the works. In August the small group of buildings in the Britannia Works which made up the Engine Test Houses were extended to form one complete building measuring 175 feet long by 77 feet 6 inches at the widest point and 31 feet wide at its narrowest point. The water cooled aero engines were tested in individual sheds, open on three sides, but for a covering of torpedo netting, and were tested using reaction torque stands rather than water or electric dynamometers.

In September the two storey Main Office building was extended 51 feet south over what had been the Brass Foundry, the original

WOLSELEY MOTORS LIMITED
EAST WORKS SITE— 1918

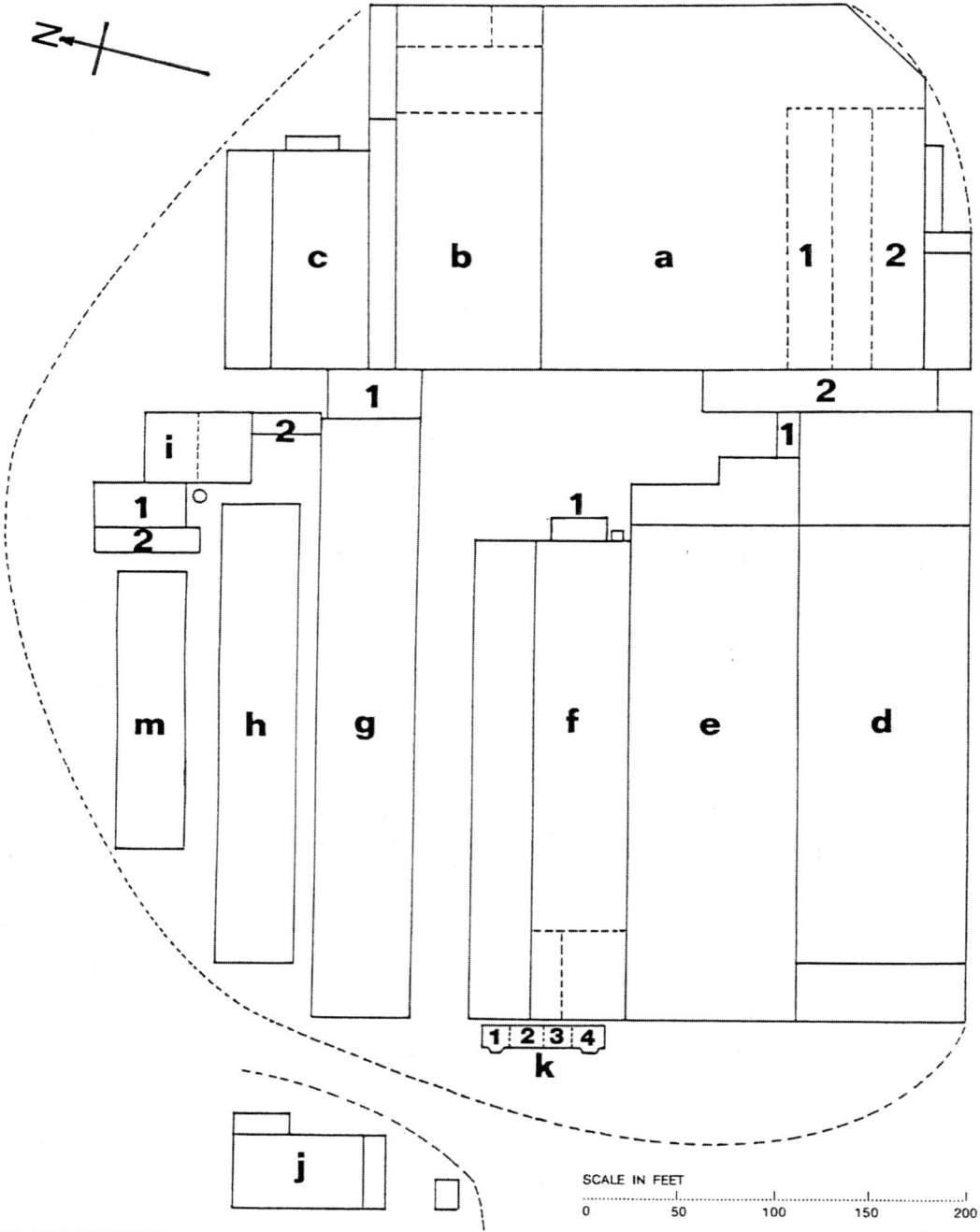

N

c b a 1 2

1
2
i
1
2

m h g f e d

1

1

2

1

1 2 3 4
k

j

SCALE IN FEET

| 0 | 50 | 100 | 150 | 200 |

BORDESLEY GREEN ROAD

EAST WORKS SITE - 1918
a. Finishing Shop.
a1. Mess Room 24ft by 144ft.
a2. Mess Room 27ft by 144ft.
b. Upholstering Shop and Varnishing Shop.
c. Body Mounting Shop.
d. Finished Car Test Shop.
e. Shell Shop.
e1. Covered Stairway from Shell Shop.
e2. Driveway between Shell Shop, Stairway, Finishing Shop, Stores and Mess Rooms roofed over.
f. Shell Shop Extension.
f1. Pump House rear of Shell Shop Extension.
g. Three storey high Paint Shop.
g1. Driveway between Paint Shop, Upholstering Shop and Body Mounting Shop roofed over.
g2. Covered way built between Paint Shop and Engine House.
h. Body Stores.
i. Engine House.
i1. Boiler House added to Engine House.
i2. Boiler House Extension.
j. Two storey high Mess Rooms.
k. Temporary Rest Rooms.
k1. Office for Welfare Supervisor.
k2. Female Rest Room.
k3. Matrons Room.
k4. Male Rest Room.

PHOTOGRAPH

The Class 'B' 30 cwt Subsidy Type vehicle based on a 'CL' type 12ft wheelbase chassis and powered by a 4 cylinder engine with a bore of 102mm diameter, stroke of 130mm, capacity of 4.25 litres, and RAC rating of 25.6 h.p. Ignition was by Bosch magneto with variable timing. A cone clutch transmitted power to the 4 speed gearbox through a short propshaft, and then to the double reduction rear axle. In chassis form it cost £635.

drawings showing that it was to be a plain building not matching the design of the original office building, but was actually built to match. However, the company reported a net profit for 1917 of £214,330.

Even during the war the Wolseley designers had obviously had time to devote to work other than armaments and patent number 115458, together with patent number 121616, dated October 25th 1917, deal with an interesting design of semi-automatic epicyclic gearbox controlled by electro-magnetic clutches.

The only addition to the East Works in 1918 was a temporary Rest Room built close to the front wall of the Shell Shop extension. This building, of timber construction, was 12 feet wide by 63 feet 6 inches long and housed separate rest rooms for men and girls, a Matrons Room and office for a Welfare Supervisor. A similar, but smaller, Rest Room was built on the Aero Site, just to the rear of the first group of houses in Bordesley Green Road. However, the Aero Site continued to expand and in 1918 a Steel Stores, 20 feet wide by 100 feet long, was added to the south wall of the Automatic Machine Shop, and a Hardening Shop, 40 feet by 60 feet, built opposite the Toolroom extension built onto the west wall of the Automatic Machine Shop in 1916. The hardening shop housed two lines of gas fired furnaces and quenching baths of water, oil and lead. The addition of these two buildings helped to make the Aero Site even more self sufficient and the only major assemblies to come from the Adderley Park works were probably the aero engines themselves. The final building to be erected on the Aero Site in 1918 was an Airship Machinery Test Shop measuring 20 feet wide by 70 feet long and housing 8 cast iron test beds each measuring 8 feet 9 inches by 3 feet 3 inches. An overhead crane ran the length of the building and there was a small office and open space for stripping down the machinery.

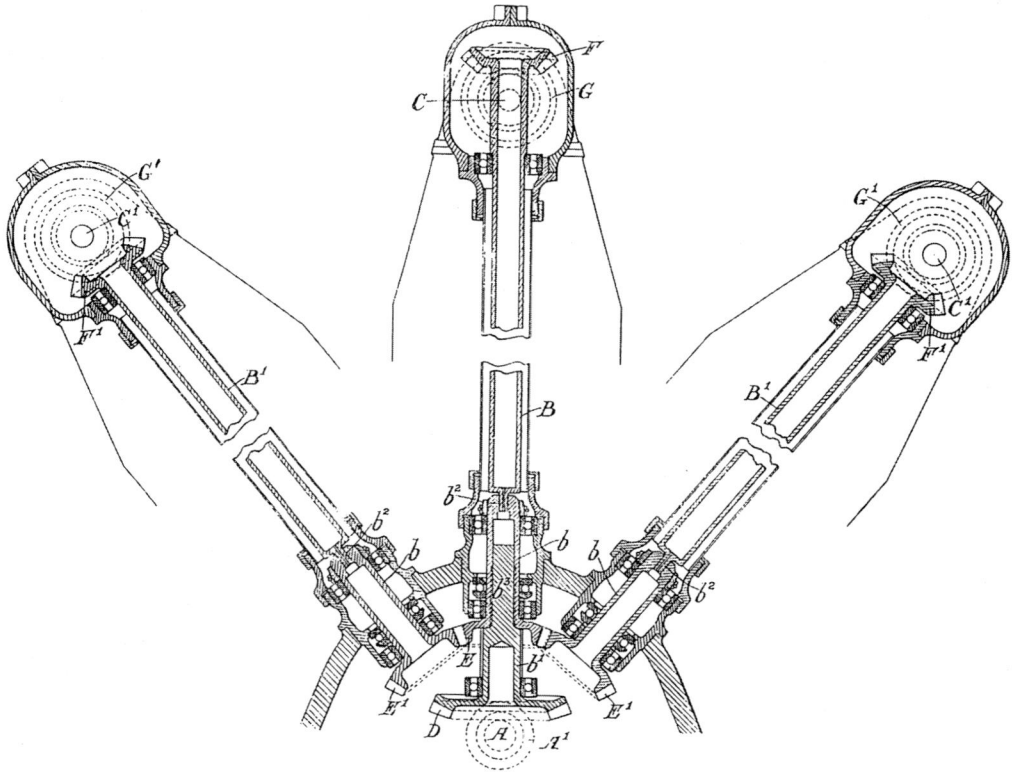

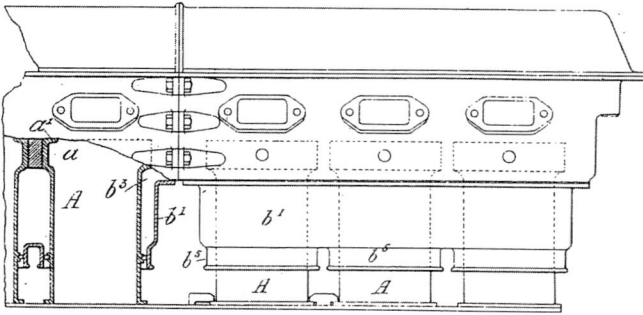

Fig. 1.

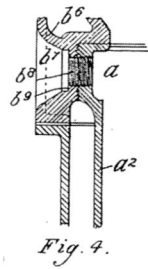

Fig. 4.

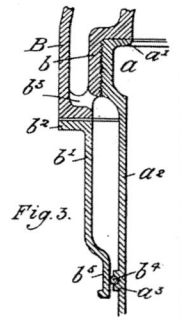

Fig. 3.

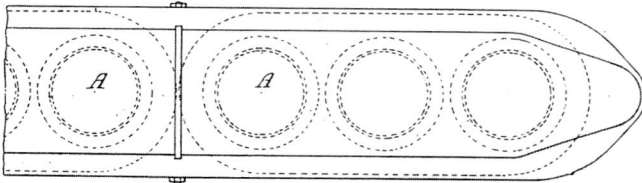

Fig. 2.

ILLUSTRATIONS

These illustrations are taken from two patents taken out in 1916 by James Davies Pitt, an engineer in the Aviation Engine Erection Shop of the company. Patent numbers 104968 and 108242 deal with the design for a triple bank water cooled engine of a type used for aircraft, or possibly, marine applications.

Each camshaft (C/C) is driven by bevel gears (F/F) from shafts (B/B). Shaft (B) is driven from the crankshaft (A) via bevel gears (A and D) which give the correct speed reduction and the drive to the camshafts for the outer cylinder banks is through bevel gears (E and E).

The lower illustrations relate to the method of constructing the cylinders, water jackets and cylinder heads using two blocks each containing three cylinders. The cylinder blocks (A) are individually fitted to a common crankcase and then finish machined in situ, Figure 1. The cylinder water jackets (b) are integral with each cylinder head, which in this instance covers three cylinders, and a rubber seal (b), Figure 3, provides a water tight seal between the water jacket and each cylinder. Figure 1 also shows how a pair of cylinder heads are bolted together to form, in this instance, a 6 cylinder, or 18 cylinder engine.

On November 11th 1918 the First World War came to an end and with it the almost instant termination of all war contracts. Companies which had switched over to the production of war material and expanded their facilities to keep up with wars insatiable appetite suddenly found themselves with no work and bigger factories to maintain than their purses could pay for. However, Wolseley had been able to continue some vehicle production throughout the war and had gained considerable experience in building technically improved engines and were now planning to produce motor cars for the peacetime market which embodied these improvements.

Only five patents were applied for in 1918, numbers 112171, 113491, 115458, 117553 and 119187, covering such subjects as, hoods for motor cars, engine camshaft drives, the control of electro-magnetic gearboxes, and carburettors. Patent number 112171 was taken out by Harold Goodwin, Carriage Designer, for improvements to 'cape-cart' type motor car hoods and patent number 117553 covers the design of a drive for overhead camshafts which incorporated both gear and chain drives, for quietness, and the extension to which could be used to drive the distributor. This latter patent is of considerable significance as the company offered 10 h.p. and 15 h.p. cars equipped with overhead camshafts immediately after the war. The 10 h.p. model was, more or less, an updated "Stellite", but now called the "Wolseley" Ten.

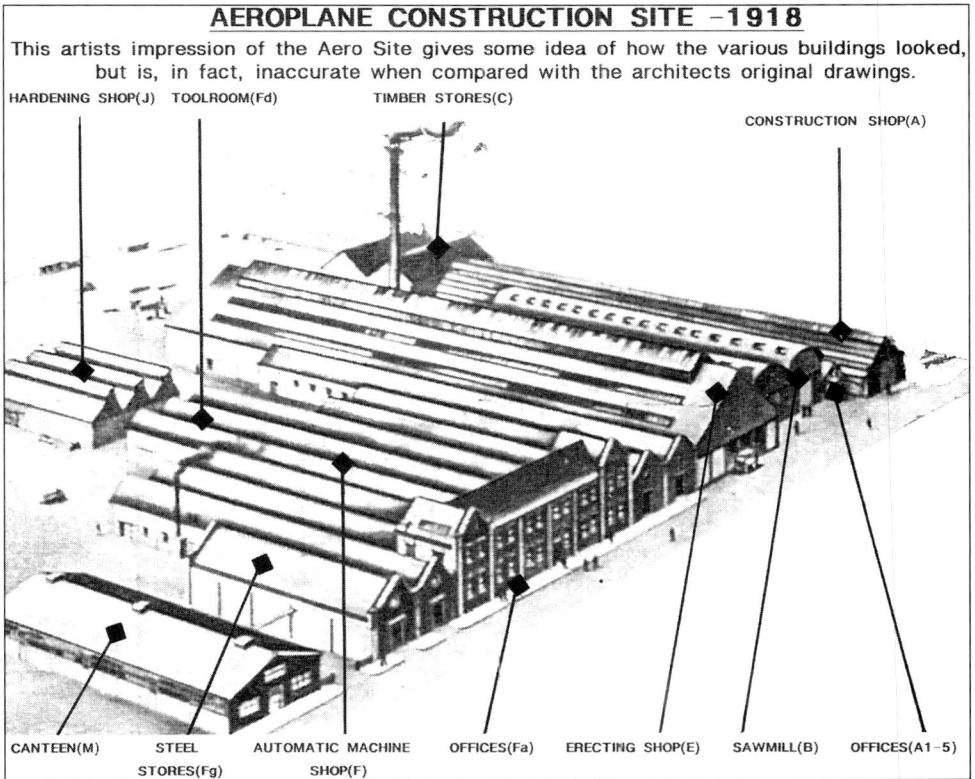

AEROPLANE CONSTRUCTION SITE –1918

This artists impression of the Aero Site gives some idea of how the various buildings looked, but is, in fact, inaccurate when compared with the architects original drawings.

HARDENING SHOP(J) TOOLROOM(Fd) TIMBER STORES(C) CONSTRUCTION SHOP(A)

CANTEEN(M) STEEL STORES(Fg) AUTOMATIC MACHINE SHOP(F) OFFICES(Fa) ERECTING SHOP(E) SAWMILL(B) OFFICES(A1–5)

WOLSELEY MOTORS LIMITED
PROPOSED DEVELOPMENT OF AERO SITE — 1919

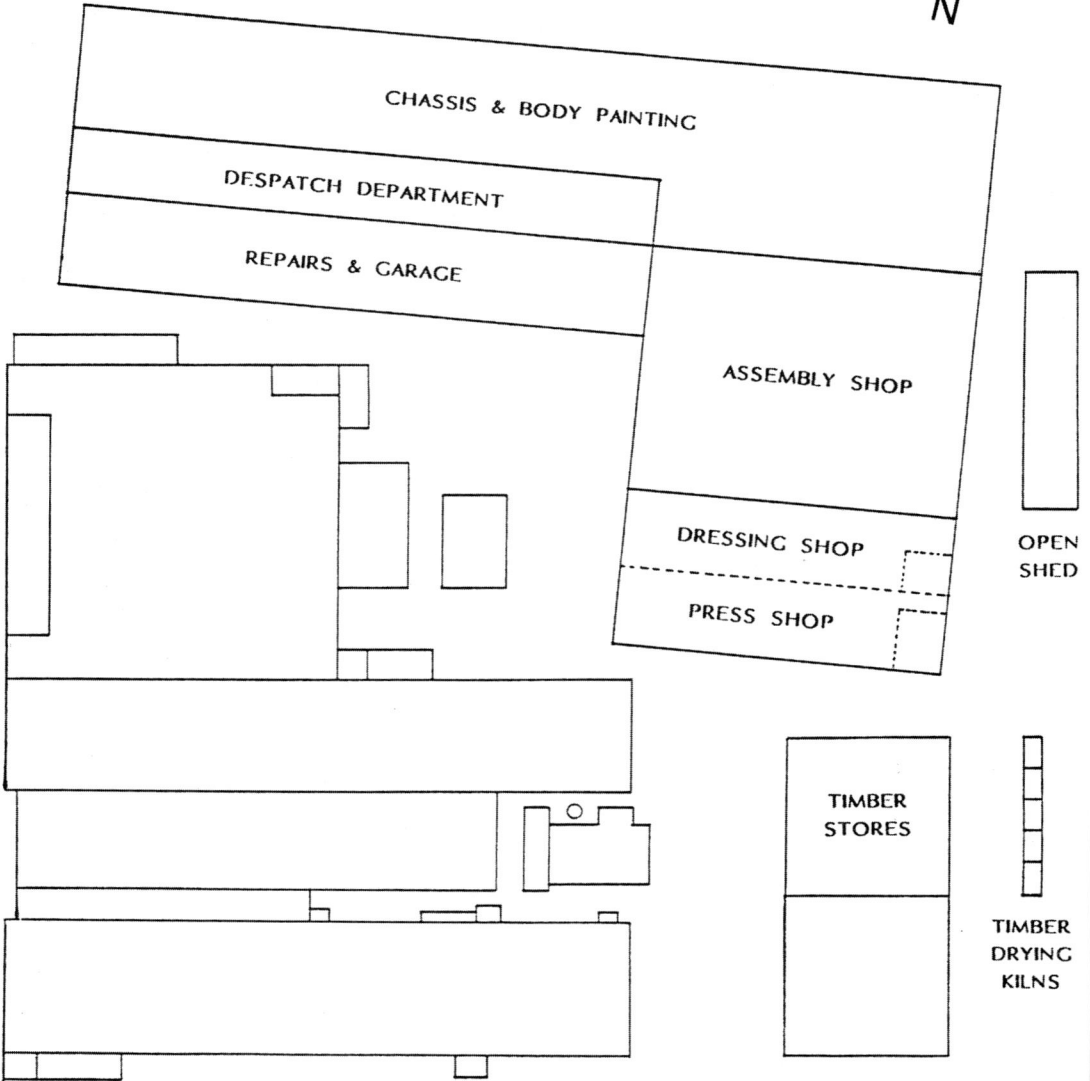

N

CHASSIS & BODY PAINTING

DESPATCH DEPARTMENT

REPAIRS & GARAGE

ASSEMBLY SHOP

DRESSING SHOP

PRESS SHOP

OPEN SHED

TIMBER STORES

TIMBER DRYING KILNS

SCALE IN FEET

| 0 | 50 | 100 | 200 | 300 | 400 |

Within a few months of the war ending the company's thoughts turned to expanding the factories to cope with the anticipated demand for motor cars which they expected would be on an even higher level than pre-war.

On April 30th, 1919 the company submitted plans to Birmingham City Council for a massive expansion of the Adderley Park and Bordesley Green factories.

In the West Works the two storey main office building along Bordesley Green Road was to have an additional floor built on top of the existing building along its entire length taking it up to a height of 48 feet and adding 9,720 square feet of office space. The Drawing Office was to be extended above the roof of the single storey workshops to the rear of the main office building upto the open cartway of the old Starley & Westwood factory, to add 7,400 square feet of space. Also to be built above the roof of the workshops was an office complex 60 feet wide by 208 feet long, connected to the first floor of the main office building, to add a further 12,480 square feet to the offices. This development comprised a Main Office 60 feet by 60 feet, twelve offices 20 feet by 26 feet and two offices 14 feet by 26 feet, all connected by a central corridor.

The four storey Jig, Tool & Gauge Shop built in 1917 along the railway siding was to be extended by the addition of another four storey building 50 feet wide by 500 feet long and 78 feet high to give an extra 100,000 square feet of production capacity. (The top floor of this building eventually housed the production area for the manufacture and assembly of S.U. carburettors made under licence by Wolseley)

In the Britannia Works the Engine Test Houses were to be extended by 45 feet 3 inches over a length of 110 feet to join up with another building and a new two storey Smithys Shop was to be erected at the corner of Arden Road and an unadopted road which led to the Britannia Brick Works. This building was to have a 180 feet long frontage to Arden Road and a 130 feet long frontage along the unadopted road, the building being 50 feet wide along Arden Road and 100 feet wide along the shorter section. A temporary roadway was applied for alongside the new Smithys and permission was granted with the proviso that "the Corporation will not be put to the cost of removing the road in the event of a road improvement taking place at any future date". The Britannia Works was also to have another Boiler House close to the Iron Foundry measuring 60 feet by 36 feet.

On the East Works site what had previously been a temporary single storey Paint Shop/Body Store was to be replaced by a two storey Carpenters & Painters Shop measuring 40 feet wide by 240 feet long, the ground floor being designated as a store with the carpenters and painters housed on the first floor with access via an external staircase. The two temporary extensions made to the Shell Shop in 1915 were to be removed and replaced by a four storey Body Making Shop 60 feet wide by 330 feet long to give 79,200 square feet of production capacity in a building towering over all the other buildings on the site at 80 feet high and containing an internal lift 9 feet 7 inches by 11 feet 3 inches, together with an internal staircase accessing all floors.

DIAGRAM

PROPOSED DEVELOPMENT
OF AERO SITE - 1919
SITE RENAMED SOUTH WORKS.

This massive development would have involved the removal of the Airship Machinery Test House and Temporary Canteen. The Timber Stores was to be doubled in size to 100 feet by 200 feet and, built 45 feet away from its west wall was to be a group of Drying Kilns 12 feet wide by 100 feet long.

The main 'L' shaped single storey building was to be 560 feet by 380 feet covering an area of 3.19 acres. An elaborate narrow gauge rail system was planned to connect the Chassis & Body Painting Shop to the Open Shed, Dring Kilns, Timber Stores and Sawmill. Inside the Chassis and Body Paint Shop a similar rail system connected all the various preparation, primer, first and second paint coat and final finish areas to the body mounting area where finish painted bodies were to be mounted on finish painted chassis.

The Repairs & Garage part of the works would have been a test and rectification area before completed cars were passed to the Despatch Department for delivery to their customers.

The purpose of this project is thought to have been to mass produce an improved version of the "Stellite" car, renamed the "Wolseley" Ten.

Interestingly, just before the expansion plans had been submitted Arthur MacCormack, the Managing Director of Wolseley, had been approached by the London based Napier company with the idea of merging the two companies, as Napier could already see post war finiancial difficulties looming. The fact that nothing came of this idea, between two very similar companies, would suggest that MacCormack could see no immediate financial problems for Wolseley, even with their post war expansion plans already drawn up and their finance, presumably, already in the bank.

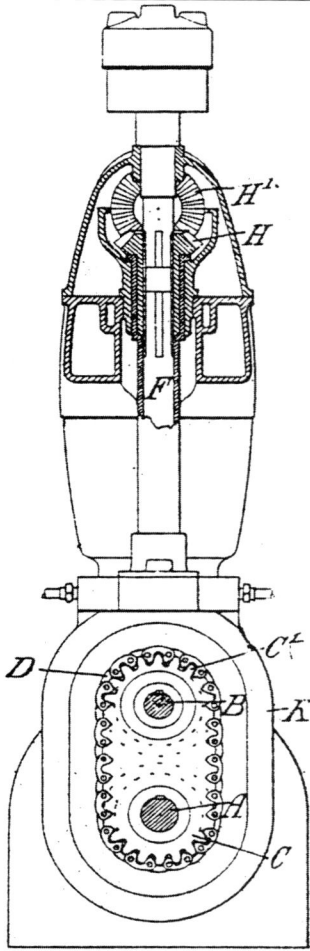

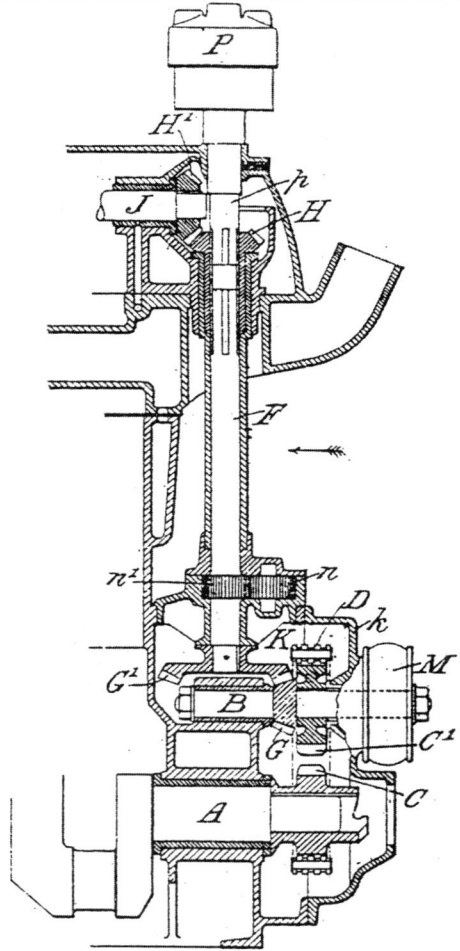

Fig. 2.

Fig. 1.

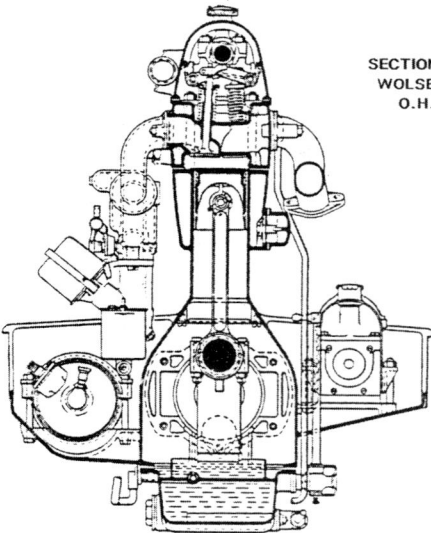

SECTIONED VIEWS OF
WOLSELEY 10 H.P.
O.H.C. ENGINE

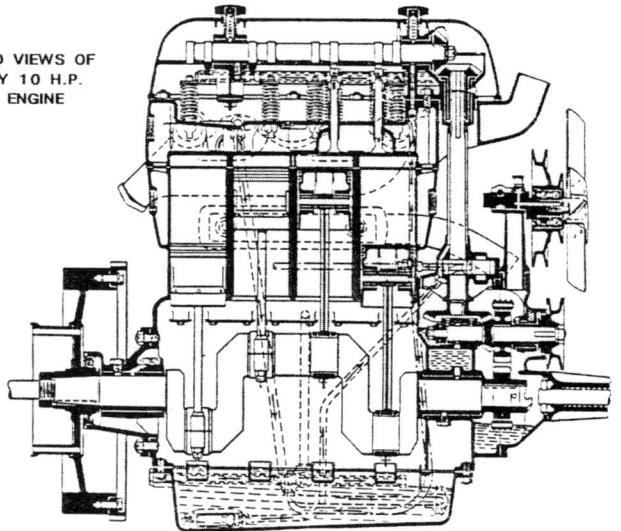

Drawings from patent number 117553, dated November 5th. 1917 and taken out jointly by Alfred Remington and Edward Reeve (Chief Draughtsman), this patent covers the design of overhead camshaft drives for a motor car engine. The use of gears to provide such a drive from the crankshaft often resulted in noise attributed to the deflection and cyclic variations of the crankshaft. This design by Wolseley aimed to reduce, if not eliminate, this source of noise by interposing a simple chain drive between the crankshaft and the reduction gear which provided the drive to the camshaft.

The lower illustrations show sectioned views of the Wolseley 10 h.p. O.H.C. engine.

PHOTOGRAPHS

Probably the first application of the patented camshaft drive was in the engine of this 1919 Wolseley Ten which featured a single overhead camshaft in the 4 cylinder unit with a bore of 65mm diameter and stroke of 95mm. The car was based on a 8ft 3ins wheelbase chassis with a track of 3ft 10ins. Fitted with a multi-disc clutch running in oil, and a rear axle containing a 3 speed gearbox and worm final drive, the car was available as a 2 or 3 seater and cost £500 or £565.

However, the largest expansion was planned for the Aero Site, now designated the South Works, where the company obviously planned to convert the site into a major motor car assembly plant in its own right, despite the fact that all the buildings erected there had been granted planning permission "for the duration of the war only".

The Timber Store, which measured 100 feet by 100 feet was to be doubled in size and alongside the new extension was to be a group of five Drying Kilns each 20 feet long by 12 feet wide. Beneath the floor of each kiln ran steam heated pipes and each kiln was to be connected to the timber store and sawmill by a series of rail tracks. An Open Shed was also to be erected on the site, 33 feet wide by 150 feet long, built from dismantled parts of the East Works Shell Shop Extension.

The largest building planned for the South Works was to be a 'L' shaped building covering an area of 3.19 acres and designated as a Press Shop, Assembly Shop and Painting & Mounting Shop. The longest section of the 'L' shape was 560 feet long and the shortest section 380 feet long. The Press Shop and Dressing Shop were each 50 feet wide by 200 feet long, the Press Shop housing a 10 ton overhead travelling crane which was to be mounted 22 feet above the shop floor of this 42 feet high part of the building. The Press Shop which was to machine press various sheet steel body panels also housed a Power Plant 30 feet by 40 feet. The Dressing Shop, used to dress, or final trim steel body panels from the Press Shop, was also to house a Sandblasting Plant 27 feet by 30 feet.

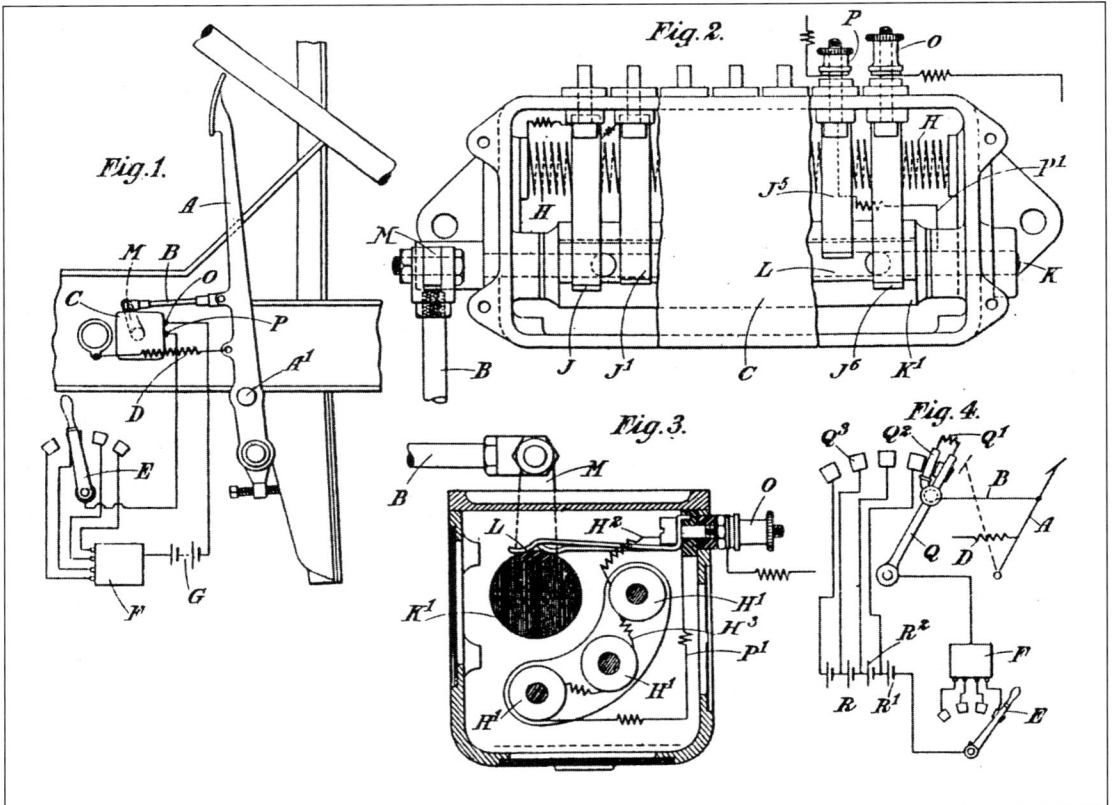

Fig. 1.

Fig. 2.

Fig. 3.

Fig. 4.

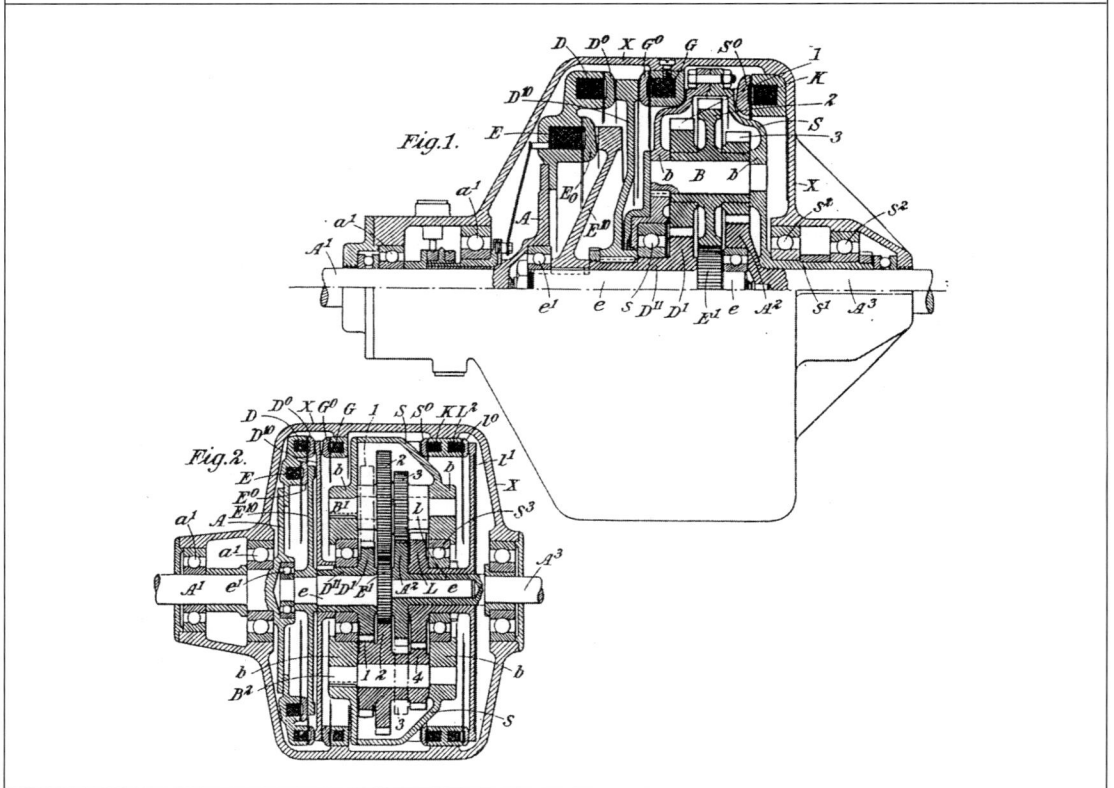

Fig. 1.

Fig. 2.

PATENT NUMBERS 115458 & 121616

Both of these patents, taken out in 1918 and 1919 respectively, deal with the design and operation of a gear change mechanism which used electro-magnetic clutches to control epicyclic gear trains. This design provided a pre-selector type of gear change in a very compact and neatly designed unit. The top diagram shows details of how the gears were selected by a hand lever 'Q', in Figure 4, which operated circuits to provide electric current to the various electro-magnetic clutches in the gearbox. Because a vehicle fitted with this type of gearbox was subject to starting off from rest with a jerk as the electro-magnetic clutch engaged, Wolseley proposed to equip vehicles with a "clutch pedal" 'A', as shown in Figure 1, which operated a series of electric resistances, Figures 2 and 3, allowing the electro-magnetic clutch for first gear to engage slowly and enabling the car to drive off smoothly. This "clutch pedal" operation was only required when the vehicle was initially starting off and all subsequent gear changes could be made by moving the gear selector lever only.

The lower diagram illustrates a three speed and reverse unit in Figure 1 and a four speed and reverse unit in Figure 2. In both designs the actual gear trains are contained within an enclosed casing which could be filled with a suitable lubricant, whilst the electro-magnetic clutches operated outside this casing and could, likewise, be supplied with a separate, and more suitable, lubricant.

Patent Number 115458 was taken out by Thomas Wardell and Patent Number 121616 by Edward Reeve.

These patents are believed to be connected with the company's experimental work using the French Cotal semi-automatic gearbox. Sir Miles Thomas who became Managing Director of Wolseley in 1937, had a special 10 h.p. car chassis built powered by a 18 h.p. engine and fitted with a Cotal gearbox, but this proved to be anything but successful, and the idea was dropped, showing that nearly 20 years of experimental work had been wasted.

The Assembly Shop measured 160 feet by 200 feet and was divided into sections for Side Panels, Back Panels, Welding Back Panels, Dickey Seat, Dash, Doors & Seat Panels and a Viewing Area. A conveyor belt 96 feet long was to feed components from the dressing shop into the assembly shop. This method of assembly was to be a complete break with the hitherto normal Wolseley practice where bodies were substantially of timber construction, but the new method of construction would undoubtedly have enabled much higher volumes to have been produced.

The Paint Shop was 560 feet long by 80 feet wide at the east end and 120 feet wide at the west end. The floor of this building was to be covered by an elaborate system of rails to connect sections like flatting areas, primer area and first and second coat areas suggesting that chassis and bodies would be mounted on wheeled bogies which went through each of the preparation and paint stages before going to the Mounting Shop, 78 feet by 60 feet, situated in one corner of the paint shop where bodies would have been mounted on to chassis.

Also to be included in this massive building was a Repairs & Garage Department, (where cars would be rectified after road testing before going to the Despatch Department) measuring 60 feet wide by 360 feet long and the Despatch Department itself which measured 40 feet wide by 360 feet long. Apart from the Press Shop and Dressing Shop the rest of this single storey building was to be 26 feet 6 inches high.

This expansion programme was obviously initiated by the company's great expectations for post war motor car sales and this massive new building on the South Works is thought to have been for the mass production of the "Wolseley" Ten, an updated version of the popular "Stellite" light car which had previously been built by the Electric & Ordnance Accessories Company Limited to Wolseley's design.

Wolseley also planned to build a new Showroom in Piccadilly, London, called Wolseley House, at a cost of about £250,000 which would epitomize the company's pre-war standing as Britains biggest motor car manufacturing company.

WOLSELEY MOTORS LIMITED
FINAL LAYOUT OF SOUTH WORKS — 1920

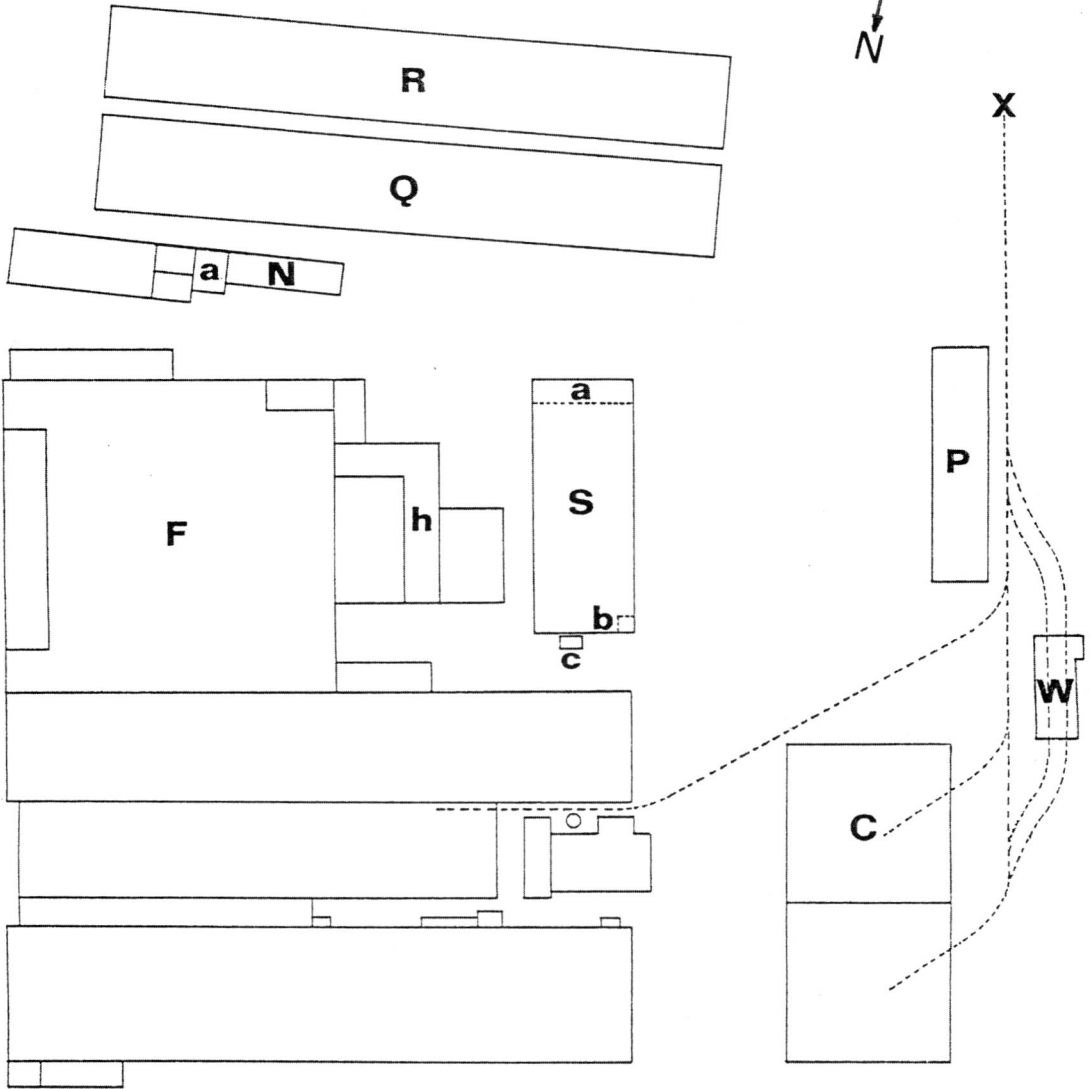

SCALE IN FEET

0   50   100   200   300   400

DIAGRAM

SOUTH WORKS - 1920

This block plan shows how the South Works (Aero Site) finally looked after all building development work had ended in 1920. Although all the buildings on this site had been built with a temporary license "for the duration of the war", most were still in use as late as 1937, many years after Wolseley had sold the site following its financial collapse in 1926.

KEY

C. Second Timber Store 100 feet by 100 feet built onto the south wall of existing Timber Store.

F. Automatic Machine Shop 200 feet by 200 feet.

Fh. Extension to Automatic Machine Shop Toolroom, connecting the Toolroom to the Hardening Shop. Built March 1920.

N. Previously the Airship Machinery Test House, this building was converted into a Millwrights Shop.

Na. A small temporary Stores 43 feet by 57 feet 6 inches was built between the Millwrights Shop and the Canteen in April 1920.

P. Open Shed 33 feet wide by 150 feet long built from parts of the dismantled Shell Shop Extension from the East Works site.

Q. Single storey Garage 61 feet wide by 375 feet long.

R. Single storey Stores 61 feet wide by 375 feet long and built 8 feet away from the south boundary of the site. Both of these buildings 'Q' and 'R' were constructed of steel frames clad with steel sheeting and were 18 feet high. Built in May 1919.

S. Single storey Coachsmiths Shop 60 feet wide by 160 feet long. Built in January 1920.

Sa. Stores area 16 feet wide by 60 feet long.

Sb. Office 10 feet 5 inches square.

Sc. Blower House of lean-to type construction, 10 feet by 14 feet added to Coachsmiths Shop in August 1920.

W. Drying Kiln. No planning application found for this building.

X. Narrow gauge rail system which connected the Open Shed (P), Drying Kiln (W), the centre of each Timber Store (C) and the Sawmill. A much more elaborate rail system had been planned for the site in 1919 with the proposal to build the massive self contained motor car assembly plant.

Whilst all the necessary planning was going on the parent company, Vickers Limited, apparently instructed Wolseley that they wished them to take over all the manufacturing facilities of the Electric & Ordnance Accessories Co. Ltd., in Ward End, Birmingham. The reason for this unexpected move by Vickers was that they, apparently, expected a substantially greater level of motor car sales post war than Wolseley and wanted Wolseley to be in a position to 'cash-in' on this trade with access to these additional facilities.

However, one suspects that there could have been a hidden ulterior motive behind this action by Vickers who now, after expanding their various factories to cope with war work, found military contracts immediately terminated with the cessation of hostilities and little in the way of post war products with which to gainfully employ their subsidiary factories. (One example of war work was that 3,027 tanks had been built, but when the war ended 10,145 more tanks were either incomplete or cancelled) By contracting their own activities and selling off subsidiary companies, like Electric & Ordnance Accessories Co. Ltd., Vickers would have put themselves into a much better position to survive, but unfortunately, at the expense of Wolseley!.

The Ward End factory in Drews Lane covered an area of 65 acres, almost twice the size of the existing Wolseley factories, and the forced acquisition of this factory made Wolseley think again about their own expansion plans at Adderley Park and Bordesley Green which have been detailed previously. The acquisition of the Electric & Ordnance Accessories Co. Ltd., cost Wolseley £400,000 and most of the planned expansion programme for the Adderley Park and Bordesley Green factories was abandoned. The only buildings actually erected were the 500 feet extension to the Jig, Tool & Gauge Shop in the Britannia Works and the Open Shed and Timber Store in South Works. The massive 'L' shaped building for the South Works had been abandoned and replaced by two single storey buildings 61 feet wide by 375 feet long to house a Store and Garage.

To help finance these projects and the re-tooling of the factories to deal with the anticipated upsurge in motor car sales a shares issue totalling £1,700,000 was agreed to by the directors of the company in November 1919.

Motor car production had started up again at Adderley Park by March and an improved version of the "Stellite" car, but still with the ash chassis frame, had been put into production at the Ward End factory of the Electric & Ordnance Accessories Co.Ltd. Improvements to the car included an uprated version of the inlet over exhaust engine with a bore of 62mm diameter and stroke of 89mm which developed 14 h.p. at 2,000 r.p.m. and fitted with an aluminium sump, a three speed gearbox with ratios of 3.32:1, 1.68:1 and 1:1, and two axle ratios of 4.9:1 for the 2 seater model and 5.4:1 for the 3 seater, with prices of £245 for a chassis and £285 for a 2 seater car. Production of this car had been moved to Ward End because the "Stellite Works" in Cheston Road had been taken over by Vickers to house the British Lighting & Ignition Co.Ltd. This company had been formed by Vickers in 1917 after the acquisition of the Bosch magneto business in Tottenham Court Road, London,

when Vickers were granted the right to use 38 Bosch patents taken out between 1908 and 1915 when they were considered as an 'enemy' company. Timken bearings had up to this time been manufactured by the Electric & Ordnance Accessories Co.Ltd., in their Aston works, but In 1915 part of the new Ward End factory was re-equipped with huge power presses and other machinery to produce these bearings, and in 1920 Vickers officially formed a new independent company, British Timken Ltd., with a capital of £50,000.

Such was the integrity of the Wolseley company that they were also building, in 1919, 16/20 h.p., 24/30 h.p. and 30/40 h.p. cars to fulfil orders placed by customers in 1915 and never delivered because of war work. Specifications for these models were still available from the company, but no new orders were being accepted.

During this eventful year the company had applied for twelve patents, numbers 121610, 122772, 124040, 126784, 127628, 128020, 129685, 132349, 132959, 135700, 136216 and 136226, covering such subjects as gearboxes, cooling of air cooled engines, variable valve gear for aircraft engines, sheet metal road wheels, grinding wheels and ordnance sighting gear. The sighting gear was developed during the war and enabled rapid tracking of aircraft for anti-aircraft guns.

The motor car range for 1920 consisted of just three basic models, 10 h.p. 1,264 c.c. 4 cylinder on a 8ft 3ins wheelbase chassis, 15 h.p. 2,574 c.c. 4 cylinder on a 9ft 10ins wheelbase chassis and a 20 h.p. 6 cylinder on a 11ft 5ins wheelbase chassis, all with worm drive rear axles, with the two smaller models featuring overhead camshaft engines and three speed gearboxes and the 20 h.p. model having a side valve engine and four speed gearbox.

The 10 h.p. car was available as a Two Seater, Three Seater or Coupe; the 15 h.p. was available as a Touring Car, Saloon or Coupe and the 20 h.p. was available as a Touring Car, Landaulette, Coupe or Limousine.

An excellent review of a Wolseley Fifteen motor car was published in "The Morning Post", written by H. Massac Buist. The author had driven the car for some 2,500 miles and was able to give a more accurate account of the vehicle than was normally possible in brief road tests carried out by other members of the press.

"Very few makers have broken with convention. Fewer still who have done so are of any reputation and have adequate resources. The most conspicuous example in this country, if not in the world, is Vickers' motor manufacturing concern, the Wolseley Company. In the 15.6 h.p. 4 cylinder overhead valve engined model with entirely new style chassis and suspension scheme it has brought forward a vehicle the progressive design of which has attracted the favourable attention of automobile engineers throughout the world."

Talking about his extended testing of the car, from Cornwall to the North of England, he adds. "The result proved conclusively that there are vast possibilities in regard to breaking with conventional practice. The vehicle brings hitherto unattained degrees of refinement, acceleration, and economy within the range of the motorist of strictly moderate means." The Dunlop Magnum tyres were said "to have merely had the freshness taken off them, and to be good for, certainly, 6,000 miles more at the revealed rate of wear" (The

PHOTOGRAPHS

A selection of Wolseley products from the 1921 range of vehicles.

TOP: A model Fifteen 4 seater enclosed Saloon which cost £1,025. Based on a 9ft 10ins wheelbase chassis this model was fitted with a 4 cylinder overhead camshaft engine, 3 speed gearbox and worm drive rear axle. The Fifteen was available in chassis form at £615, a 2 seater open Touring Car at £795, a 4 seater Sporting Model with polished aluminium bodywork at £900 and as a 6 seater Town Carriage, with open driving compartment, at £1,150.

CENTRE: A Wolseley 'Fifteen' in chassis form showing how much it resembled the small 'Ten' model, having a similar suspension system, but fitted with a conventionally mounted 3 speed gearbox, and with the petrol tank mounted across the rear of the chassis frame. The overhead camshaft engine had a bore of 3.125" diameter and stroke of 5.125", giving it a capacity of 2,574 c.c.

BOTTOM: A Wolseley Twenty model fitted with a 4 seater Coupe De Luxe body with folding roof allowing it to be converted into an open car and priced at £1,500. The power unit was a 6 cylinder side valve engine rated at 23.5 h.p., was based on a 11ft 5ins wheelbase chassis and was fitted with a 4 speed gearbox driving into a worm drive rear axle. In chassis form the cost was £950 and it was also available as a 4 seater Touring Car, as a 4 seater Sporting model, a 4 seater Landaulette with folding seats for two more passengers, and as a Limousine with similar seating arrangements at a cost of £1,500.

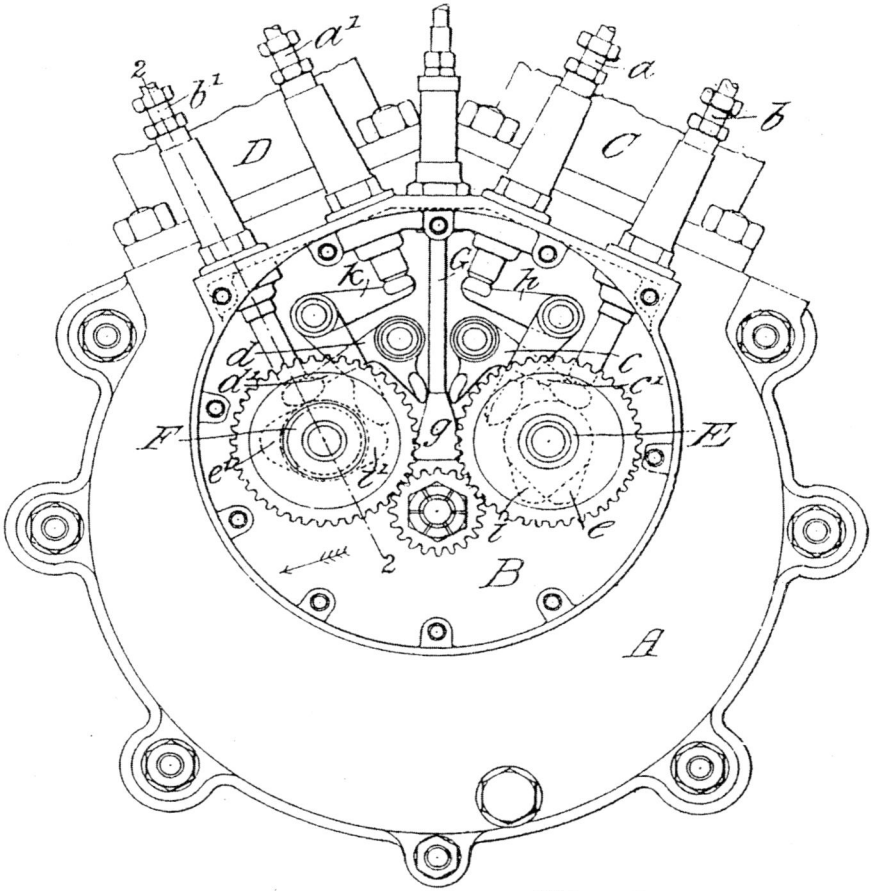

Fig. 1.

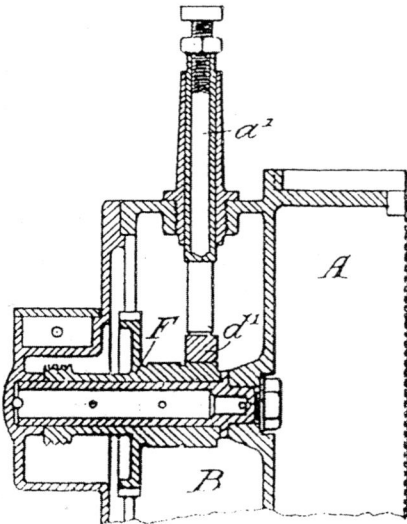

Fig. 2.

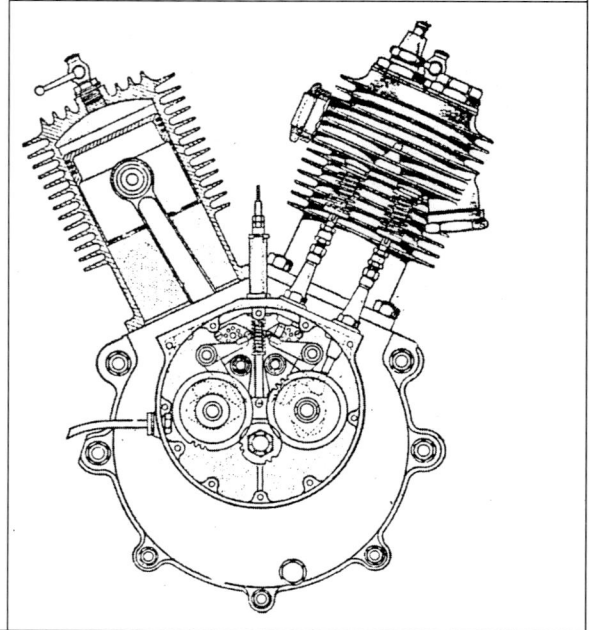

car had by this time covered a total of 3,900 miles) "Apart from the light weight of the car, the ease on tyres is due to the patented system of suspension, wherein there is the minimum of unsprung weight, and with which it is possible to ride over given roads at 10 m.p.h. faster than cars of conventional construction are able to take them with equivalent comfort."

The suspension was comprised of leading, cantilevered inverted quarter elliptics to the front and trailing, cantilevered inverted quarter elliptics to the rear, a type of suspension used widely by many motor car manufacturers, but Remington had somehow managed to 'tune' the suspension so finely to the weight of the car that it produced exceptional ride and handling qualities.

"The power of the engine is remarkable when driven on petrol; on a mixture of half petrol and half benzol it is astonishing. When the car has got under way along the level, by advancing the spark one can get almost the same effect as in other cars is obtained by opening the throttle fully. I have never known a standard engine to answer so pronouncedly to ignition variation. That makes for economy. The engine balance approximates to perfection so closely that one cannot detect any period (hesitation) at any speed or load." The immediate response of the overhead camshaft engine to the ignition being advanced was also commented on favourably in test reports of the smaller Wolseley Ten.

"This is a car which travels at from 5 to 53½ m.p.h. on the top gear, on which the acceleration is so pronounced that you can make a high mean speed from point to point across country with relatively low maximum speed."

The braking system was commented on thus. "Both sets act on the rear wheels, they are equally powerful; either can pull the car up in a remarkably short space; yet both are very smooth in action."

Summing up his report he adds. "The result leaves one entirely satisfied that our largest motor manufacturing firm is thoroughly justified in its daring policy. The charm of the car grows on one the further one drives it. For its accommodation and performance certainly it is the most economical of tyres, fuel, and lubricant in my experience." Owner drivers were reporting average fuel consumption of these cars at 23 to 24 m.p.g. during normal every day use.

Then comes, perhaps, the most revealing statement in this report. "The trial I have made gives me the explanation of the very studious attention the American industry is paying to this example of British pioneering in motor car evolution, for this is a vehicle one is unable to compare with any other on the world's market in that it is wholly original and furnishes at a moderate cost desirable qualities of performance hitherto unobtainable. In that sense it will be found that the Wolseley Company is making motoring history."

Mr S.F.Edge, writing in "The Auto Motor Journal" also wrote favourably about this car. "The 15 h.p. four cylinder Wolseley is a model which nobody can ignore. It is super efficient, and gives travel-service of a class that few cars can equal, much less excel".

And yet, the car did not sell in anything like the numbers expected of it. It was, perhaps, too ahead of its time, and it was of course a very expensive motor car, costing £615 in chassis form. However, the comment about the American car industry taking an interest in the new Wolseley cars is quite revealing, especially when one learns that an American company was actually bidding for the company when it went into receivership five years later.

ILLUSTRATION

PATENT NUMBER 154268

This patent is of particular interest as Wolseley manufactured vee twin motor cycle engines from 1921 for the Royal Enfield company. The patent was taken out in July 1919 by Edward Reeve and Edward Luyks, a Superintendent with the company.

The patent relates to the operation of the valve gear for a vee twin engine. In Figure 1 the engine crankcase 'A' contains an inner casing 'B' which houses the camshafts, 'E' and 'F' which are driven at half crankshaft speed. The base of each cylinder can be seen at 'C' and 'D', together with the inlet valve tappets 'a' and 'a' and exhaust tappets 'b' and 'b'. The camshaft 'E' has an inlet cam 'i' and exhaust cam 'e' whilst the camshaft 'F' has an inlet cam 'i' and exhaust cam 'e'. Bell crank levers 'c' and 'd' are pivoted close to the centre line of the crankcase and have short arms operated by the two camshafts which in turn operate the exhaust tappets via their long arms. Bell crank levers 'h' and 'k' are pivoted between the two sets of tappets and have their long arms operated by the inlet cams which in turn operates the inlet tappets 'a' and 'a' via their short arms. The vertical rod 'G' on the centre line of the engine has at its lower end a wedge shape 'g' which, when the rod is lifted remotely via a Bowden cable, presses apart the short arms of the exhaust bell cranks 'c' and 'd', thereby opening the exhaust valves.

INSET: A part cross-sectioned view of one of the actual engines made for the Royal Enfield company which incorporated the patented valve operating mechanism.

In January 1920 a Coachsmiths Shop measuring 60 feet wide by 160 feet long was built on the South Works site and in March the Automatic Machine Shop Toolroom was extended to join up with the Hardening Shop, but there was no further development of the East Works, West Works or Britannia Works and the Adderley Park and Bordesley Green factories were now to remain stagnant for the remaining years under Wolseley ownership.

However, one more development was planned in May 1920, not as part of the factory, but a Social Club to be built on a site in Alum Rock Road, just a few minutes walk from the Adderley Park Works. (Works social events had been held in the two storey Mess Rooms built on the East Works site in 1910) The building was basically 'T' shaped with the centre being two storeys high, 50 feet wide and 130 feet long and the two single storey wings 35 feet wide by 45 feet long. A Caretakers House was also to be built on the site which also contained a bowling green, football pitch and tennis courts, the latter being situated at the corner of Parkfield Road and Couchman Road. Facilities on the ground floor of the new clubhouse were to include a reception hall with ticket office, council room, lounge 25 feet by 35 feet, smoke room with bar 19 feet 6 inches by 35 feet, ladies room with servery 20 feet by 35 feet, card room 19 feet by 20 feet 9 inches, chess room 14 feet by 19 feet, billiard room containing 8 tables 50 feet by 59 feet 7 inches, bagatelle room containing 2 tables 14 feet by 25 feet, billiard room containing 1 table 25 feet by 25 feet, a dark room 10 feet by 25 feet and two dressing rooms, one for home teams and one for visiting teams, each 14 feet 3 inches by 25 feet. The upper floor comprised a stage 20 feet by 50 feet with separate dressing rooms for men and women, a large sitting area 50 feet by 70 feet and separate cloakrooms for men and women.

The financial position of the company dictated that this ambitious facility for the Wolseley workers would never be built and a revised plan was submitted in August 1921 for a single storey building constructed of timber measuring 20 feet 5 inches wide by 60 feet 8 inches long. With a bar at one end the building contained seating around the inner perimeter of the walls and just one billiard table and one bagatelle table. In March 1923 an extension of this timber building was planned measuring 20 feet 5 inches wide by 46 feet long.

(This site was purchased by Morris Commercial in November 1937 for £5,500 who built a Sports & Social Pavilion costing £20,000 which was opened by Lord Nuffield in 1939.)

One interesting development took place this year when a representative of the company, Bert Penniall, went to Tokyo to oversee the production of Wolseley commercial vehicles and motor cars at the Ishikawajima Shipbuilding & Engineering Company Ltd., the two companies having signed a licensing agreement in late 1918. A number of 10hp and 15 hp motor cars were built in 1921 and 1922, but it was to be 1924 before production of the 'CC' type one tonner and 'CP' type 30 cwts commercials began in earnest. About 560 commercial vehicles were built between 1924 and 1927, but the licensing agreement seemed to do little to assist the finances of the Wolseley company and to make matters worse Edward Reeve M.I.Mech.E., M.I.A.E., M.S.AS.E., resigned from his position as Technical Manager in January 1925 to take up an appointment as Advisor to the Japanese company.

The only commercial vehicle to be produced by the company after the First World War was this neat little 7 cwts Light Delivery Van introduced in 1921 at £400. The van appears to have been based upon the Wolseley Ten motor car chassis which had a wheelbase of 8ft 3ins and was powered by a 4 cylinder overhead camshaft engine. The suspension, as can be seen in this picture, featured leading cantilevered springs at the front and trailing cantilevered springs to the rear. The van body had an open cab with just a shallow windscreen to protect the driver from the elements and two vertically hinged rear doors giving access to the load compartment. This design, according to the sales literature, "will revolutionise light parcels deliveries".

This was not the first time that the company had formed associations with an overseas manufacturer, as a licensing agreement had been signed in 1907 with the Societa Officine Legnansi Automobili to make Wolseley-Siddeley motor cars in Legnano near Milan in Italy, but this too appeared to have been short lived and did little for the Wolseley company.

1920 had not been a good year for the company as it had lost five months production because of the national strike of moulders, but by December thirty cars per day were being built and the company was hoping for an output approaching 10,000 cars in 1921.

Even the product development appears to have come to a standstill and only three patents were applied for during 1920, numbers 141492, 153967 and 154268, covering gearboxes and valve gear for a vee twin engine. The latter is of particular interest as Wolseley built large numbers of air cooled vee-twin motor cycle engines for the Royal Enfield company in Redditch from 1921. These engines had a bore of 85.5mm diameter and stroke of 85mm giving a capacity of 964c.c and rated at about 8 h.p. and were used in their motor cycle combination outfits. A "Motor Cycle" contemporary road test described the engine as having "a delightful feeling of liveliness" and "gives a decided impression of effortlessness", with the outfit returning a fuel consumption of 50 to 55 m.p.g. over a 150 miles test route taking in the Malvern Hills.

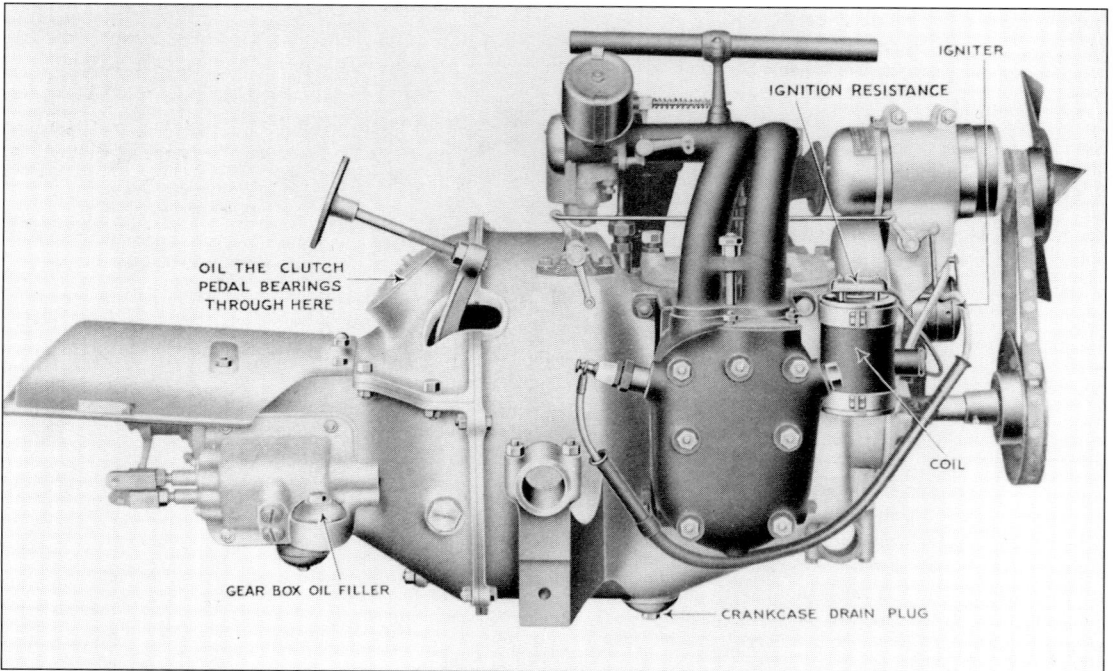

OIL THE CLUTCH
PEDAL BEARINGS
THROUGH HERE

IGNITION RESISTANCE

IGNITER

COIL

GEAR BOX OIL FILLER

CRANKCASE DRAIN PLUG

The product range for 1921 remained much the same as 1920, with 10 h.p., 15 h.p. and 20 h.p. models, but with additional body options available. The 10 h.p. car was sometimes referred to as the Wolseley-Stellite 'Ten' and was available with a Two Seater body at £475 as an economy model or with a Torpedo body at £525 and a Two Seater Coupe with fixed head at £650. The 15 h.p. was available as a Two Seater or Four Seater Touring Car at £795, a Sports Model with polished aluminium bodywork at £900, a Saloon at £1,025, a Two Seater Coupe at £995, a Four Seater Coupe at £1,135, a Single Landaulette at £1,050 or a Town Carriage at £1,150. The top of the range 20 h.p. car was available as an open Touring Car De-Luxe at £1,200, a Sporting Model De-Luxe with polished aluminium body at £1,275, a Landaulette De-Luxe at £1,450, a Limousine De-Luxe at £1,500 and a Four Seater Coupe De-Luxe at the same price. The 1921 cars all featured battery ignition systems supplied by the British Lighting & Ignition Co.Ltd.

Additionally, a small 7 cwt light delivery van, with open cab, was introduced priced at £400 based upon a 10 h.p. car chassis.(This may have been based on the 1915 "Stellite" van design)

The company now employed 8,000 workers (3,000 more than their wartime workforce), had a production capacity of 12,000 cars per year and was currently building 150 cars per week. The motor industry appeared to be picking up as 8,449 cars and chassis had been exported in 1920 worth £6,404,332 compared with 2,191 cars and chassis worth £1,526,096 exported in 1919, petrol consumption had risen from 713,883,000 gallons to 876,027,000 gallons and revenue from vehicle licensing stood at £11,000,000 with 870,782 motor vehicles licensed in Britain. In 1921 3,016 motor cars/chassis had been exported, worth £2,597,214 and 9,209 motor cars/chassis imported, worth £2,384,590.

In September 1921 Alfred Remington left the company, because of illness, but started up his own business as a consultant engineer with premises in New Eldon Chambers, Cherry Street, Birmingham. (In March 1922 Remington delivered his paper to the Institute of Automobile Engineers entitled "The Design & Functioning of Laminated Automobile Suspension Springs", but in July of the same year he died)

In September the company announced plans to build a 7 h.p. motor car powered by a horizontally opposed twin cylinder engine with a bore of 82mm diameter and stroke of 92mm. With a wheelbase of 8ft 1in and track of 3ft 8ins the car weighed about 9½ cwts and had a top speed of about 40 m.p.h. When the 7 h.p. two seater car was introduced it sold well and was awarded a gold medal at its first public appearance competing in the Scottish Six Days Reliability Trial. Wolseley products were still highly regarded by owners and one owner from Bournemouth wrote in 1921, " *I should like to say how pleased I am with the Wolseley 10 h.p. car, delivered by you last December. I have done about 2,300 miles without any troubles, and last week, after a run of 102 miles, found the amount of petrol and benzol used worked out at 43 miles to the gallon. The next day 90 miles gave the same result. Both days were spent in fairly hilly country, and were rather cold, so that warm weather may have given even a better mileage to the gallon. I might*

PHOTOGRAPHS

TOP: The little "Wolseley" Seven 2 seater motor car based on a 8ft 1in wheelbase chassis which weighed just 7 cwt without the body and the car had a top speed of about 37 m.p.h. The 3 speed gearbox was bolted direct to the engine and drove the spiral bevel rear axle via an open propshaft. The brakes were comprised of fabric lined shoes expanding in drums on the rear axle only, operated by the footbrake and handbrake lever.

The price, in 1922, was £255 plus an extra £15 for a starter motor and an extra £9 when fitted with the full width windscreen as shown here.

BOTTOM: The power unit for the Seven was this very neat and compact 2 cylinder engine with horizontally opposed cylinders, and was the first horizontal engine produced by the company for about 14 years. This water cooled engine had a bore of 82mm diameter and stroke of 92mm, was rated at 8.5 h.p., but actually produced a maximum of 14 b.h.p. at the top end of its speed range of 500 r.p.m. to 2,500 r.p.m. The manifolding took exhaust gases across the engine to a forward facing downpipe where the patented automatic equalising carburettor was fitted, fuel being gravity fed from the scuttle mounted 4 gallon tank. The method of driving the dynamo and distributor on this engine had been patented by the company in patent number 186518, taken out in September 1921.

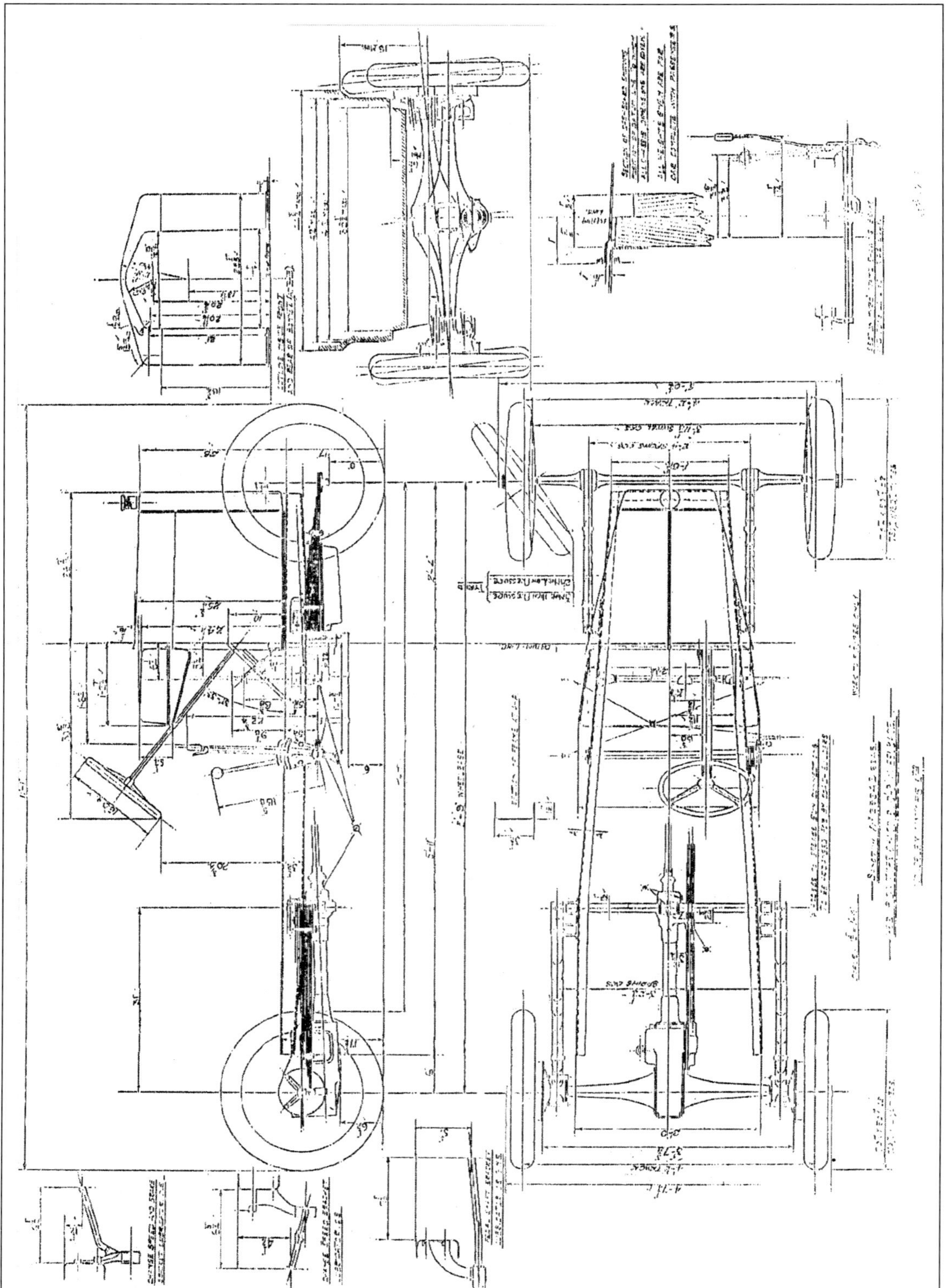

add that the small consumption did not in any way detract from the sweet running of the car. I got her up to 42 m.p.h. quite easily, and think she would have done more if the road had been fit for it, and she climbed wonderfully well, doing almost every ordinary hill on top and the remainder on second gear."

In December a streamlined car based upon the 1261cc 10 h.p. chassis and driven by Captain A.G. Miller and Mr G.A. Vandervell set up ten new records at Brooklands when the car ran for 6 hours and 15 minutes and covered a total distance of 514 miles and 1,124 yards achieving 250 miles at an average of 82 m.p.h., 300 miles at an average of 82.54 m.p.h., 400 miles at an average of 82.55 m.p.h. and 500 miles at an average of 81.79 m.p.h.

Only two patents were applied for in 1921, numbers 156474 and 162853, covering engine lubrication and carburettors.

In May 1922 a modified "Wolseley" Ten with streamlined bodywork and weighing 1,536 lbs set up new endurance records at Brooklands when it covered a distance of 843 miles at an average speed of 70.32 m.p.h. during a 12 hours non stop run, followed by a further 12 hours run the next day to cover a total distance of 1,456.6 miles at an average speed of 61.06 m.p.h. and with a fastest lap of 79.05 m.p.h. This record attempt had been dogged by atrocious weather conditions and some mechanical breakdowns and the driving had been shared this time by Captain A.G. MIller, Mr. C.F. Temple and Mr. G.A. Vandervell. However, a Wolseley entered in the Brooklands 200 mile race in August driven by Captain Miller did not do so well and finished 8th in its class at an average speed of 66.2 m.p.h.

In September a 15 h.p. Wolseley with an engine capacity of 2,771cc established 39 records for a Class D motor car at Brooklands, some of the records included 1 hour covering a distance of 87 miles 1,517 yards at 87.85 m.p.h., 5 hours covering a distance of 438 miles 272 yards at 87.63 m.p.h., 10 hours covering a distance of 842 miles 1,338 yards at 84.27 m.p.h. and 12 hours covering a distance of 1,015 miles 1,234 yards at an average speed of 84.62 m.p.h. The car returned an incredible 16 m.p.g. and replicas of the record breaking car were immediately made available by the company at £700 to any prospective buyer.

This was not the end of Wolseley's record breaking in 1922, as a special four cylinder 2 litre car, with a bore of 77.8mm diameter and stroke of 104.87mm was built to take records for Class B cars at Brooklands. Driven by Captain Miller and Mr. L.C. LeChampion the car established new records of 400 miles at 78.49 m.p.h., 500 miles at 78.29 m.p.h., 600 miles at 78.77 m.p.h., 700 miles at 78.94 m.p.h., 800 miles at 78.61 m.p.h. and 900 miles at an average speed of 78.8 m.p.h. bringing the year on the track to a triumphant conclusion.

Two new models were added to the range of cars for 1923, a a 14 h.p. and a 24/30 h.p. The latter model was powered by a six cylinder engine with a bore of 90 mm diameter, stroke of 140mm with a capacity of 5.344 cc, based on a 11ft 8ins wheelbase chassis, fitted with a four speed gearbox and worm drive rear axle, this appeared to be Wolseley's return to the large motor car market where it had really excelled in pre war days. The 14 h.p. car was powered by a four cylinder side valve engine with a bore of 80mm diameter and stroke of 130mm with a capacity of 2,614cc to cater for motorists who had been unwilling to buy the 15 h.p. model fitted with the more modern overhead camshaft engine. Based on the same 9ft 10ins wheelbase

ILLUSTRATION

This reproduction from a rather faded works drawing shows the chassis for a long wheelbase version of the "Wolseley" Ten. The standard model had a wheelbase of 8ft 3ins, but for the Light Four Seater the wheelbase was extended by 6ins and the front wheel track increased by 4ins to provide additional room to accomodate four passengers instead of two. The car itself was available in basic form at £400, or with a higher specification at £425. The four cylinder overhead camshaft engine produced a maximum of 21 b.h.p. and featured a chain and gear drive to the camshaft.

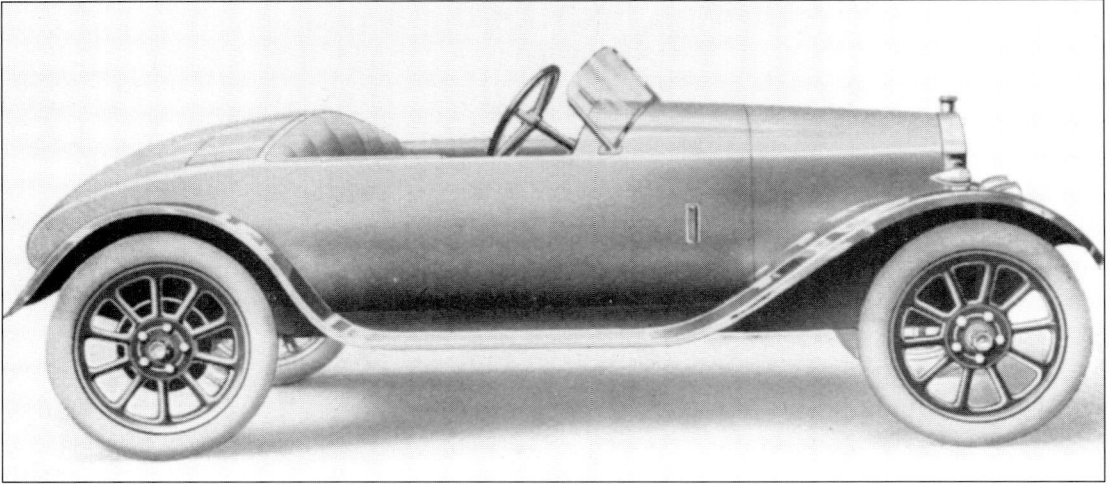

chassis as the 15 h.p. model it also featured a three speed gearbox and worm drive rear axle. Only three patents were taken out in 1922, numbers 177089, 185959 and 186518 all dealing with engines. The spirit of inovation and drive appears to have been taken out of the company and it seemed to be trundling along trying to live solely upon its past reputation. The loss of a designer like Remington could have had some bearing on the product development, but the company was obviously already experiencing financial difficulties and the country itself was heading into an unexpected depression. Financial results for 1921/22 were also depressing with a net loss of £97,030, but Sir Vincent Caillard did make public that an engineers strike between March and June of 1922 had lost the company about £300,000 in its annual turnover.

In February 1923 the "Brooklands Speed Model" was announced being a replica of the 10 h.p. car which had taken part in the Brooklands 200 mile race. Priced at £695 the car was guaranteed to reach a speed of 65 m.p.h. over a standing mile.

The car range for 1924 consisted of a 7 h.p. two cylinder model, 10 h.p. four cylinder model, 14 h.p. and 15 h.p. four cylinder models based upon the same 9' 10" wheelbase chassis but with the 14 h.p. model having a three speed gearbox and worm drive rear axle and the 15 h.p. having a four speed gearbox and spiral bevel rear axle. The remaining two models were a 20 h.p. six cylinder model on a 11' 5" wheelbase chassis and the 24-30 h.p. model six cylinder model on a 11' 8" wheelbase chassis frame.

During 1923 Britain had imported 327,233,737 gallons of petrol at a cost of £15,827,394, had imported 16,617 complete motor cars and 12,637 motor car chassis at a total cost of £4,494,656 and had exported 3,259 complete motor cars and 2,023 chassis worth a total of £2,187,210.

No patents were taken out in 1923 or 1924, but in February 1924 Mr Arthur McCormack the Managing Director resigned from the company and was replaced by Mr Bernard Caillard and Mr Alexis Jacob. This arrangement lasted but a few months after which a Committee of Management was set up comprising Mr. M.B.U. Dewar as Chairman, together with Mr B.Caillard, Mr W. Dallow and Mr. G.W. Grazebrook. Interestingly, Mr F.W. Lanchester the brilliant motor car designer and engineer was appointed as consulting engineer to collaborate design work with the Wolseley Technical Manager Mr. Edward Reeve. Lanchester's contribution to the company, if any, has not been recorded, other than a recollection by a past employee that an experimental engine with an unusual firing order was built to his design, but never put into production.

In April Woolf Barnato driving a Wolseley 10 h.p. car won the Brooklands 27th 75 m.p.h. Handicap Race of 8½ miles at a speed of 79.25 m.p.h. This success was followed up in June by a Wolseley "Viper" car, powered by a Wolseley 11.76 litre V8 aero engine which set new records up to 6 hours at Brooklands including 250 kilometres record at 85.37 m.p.h. and 3 hours record covering a distance of 161 miles 706 yards at an average speed of 53.08 m.p.h. The car was privately entered and driven by Captain A.G.Miller and Mr. G.N.Norris.

No financial results were reported for 1924, but no dividends had been paid to shareholders which gives some indication of the company's financial position.

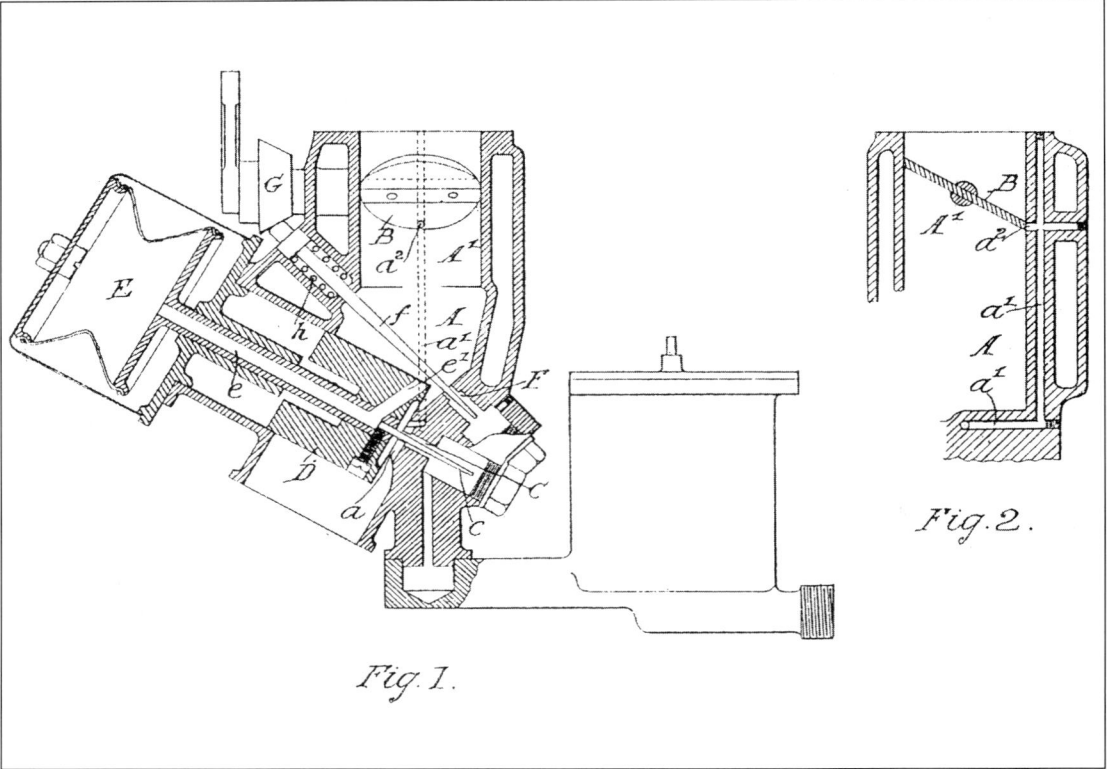

Fig. 1.

Fig. 2.

For 1925 the range of cars was trimmed down and comprised a 11/22 h.p., 16/35 h.p., 15/40 h.p. and a 24/55 h.p. model, the smallest having a four cylinder engine with a bore of 65mm diameter and stroke of 95mm, the rest having engines with a bore of 80mm diameter and stroke of 130mm, the 24/55 h.p. model being a six cylinder. However, the 16/35 and 24/55 now featured four wheel brakes, monobloc cylinder castings and detachable cylinder heads.

The company also took on work for other companies, such as manufacturing 4.3 litre four cylinder engines for the "Midland Red", or Birmingham & Midland Motor Omnibus Company Ltd., as it was more correctly named. The engine was a fairly conventional side valve design with a cast aluminium crankcase, cast iron cylinder blocks in pairs, two piece pistons, and with aluminium cylinder heads designed by Harry Ricardo. The deep aluminium sump had an oil pump externally mounted and driven by an open vertical shaft from the camshaft. With a bore of 105mm diameter, stroke of 125mm and a 5.6:1 compression ratio the performance was said to be 'like a well tuned sports car'.

Only two patents were taken out in 1925, numbers 231348 and 140608, dealing with gearboxes and races for roller bearings respectively. During the following year four patents were applied for, numbers 245563, 246246, 248032 and 261488, covering brakes, motor car hoods and gearboxes.

In February 1926 a new model was announced, the 11-22 h.p. which featured a modified overhead camshaft engine with all gear drive and the dynamo and magneto fitted transversely across the front of the engine driven by a worm gear from the vertical shaft drive to the overhead camshaft. The modified engine was designated the "All Gear" type to distinguish it from the earlier chain/gear drive originally patented by the company. In a contemporary road test the new model was found to have a top speed of 50 m.p.h., could accelerate from 10 m.p.h. to 30 m.p.h. in 22 seconds in top gear, or in 13 seconds in second gear, and returned a creditable 33 m.p.g. from its 1261 c.c. engine. Another new car was announced in September, a 16-45 h.p., powered by a new six cylinder overhead camshaft engine with a bore of 65mm diameter and stroke of 101mm giving it a capacity of 2025cc.(This became known as the "Silent Six") With a four speed gearbox, bevel drive rear axle and 9' 9" wheelbase chassis frame the new model was available with a saloon body at £495, or with a touring body at £450.

Sir Herbert Austin probably recalled his days at Wolseley as news of the company's financial situation circulated within the motor industry, particularly in July 1926 when the Austin Motor Company celebrated its 21st anniversary with 20,000 staff, employees, employees families and guests attending a huge ceremony at Longbridge where they were building about 450 cars per week and had returned a gross profit of £748,890-2s-6d during the last financial year. Austin must also have been thinking of his efforts in June 1924 to amalgamate the Austin, Morris and Wolseley companies into one to achieve some sort of rationalisation and economy of production to meet the expected stiff Post War competition. However, Morris had rejected this overture by Austin virtually out of hand and Wolseley's reaction is not known, but Austin was to try

ILLUSTRATION

Drawings from patent number 119187, taken out jointly by Edward Reeve and Alfred Remington in February 1918. The 'S.U.' type of carburetter had been manufactured by the company for some time and used widely on its products, but obviously had some problems associated with its use, particularly in cold starting and slow running. This patent was designed to address both of these problems by increasing the velocity of the air across the jet causing the surface tension on the fuel to break and allow more fuel to flow from the jet than in standard form. This was achieved by drilling a small diameter passageway from the point where the throttle disc, or butterfly 'B', closed, or substantially closed, onto the wall of the carburetter 'A' at point a' to a point just inwards of the main jet 'C'. This enabled a slightly richened mixture to be created for starting and slow running. (Later designs of the 'S.U.' carburetter provided a means of lowering the jet mechanically to achieve a richer mixture).

A further improvement to the 'S.U' design was proposed by the addition of an auxiliary jet 'F' operated mechanically by the coil spring 'h' and cam 'G' on the throttle spindle to provide a richer mixture when the throttle was fully open, but the engine under full load and running at relatively slow revolutions.

PHOTOGRAPH

Close up view of the 1923 4 cylinder side valve 14 h.p. engine introduced to appease buyers reluctant to accept the far more technically advanced single overhead camshaft engines being used by the company in their range of small cars at this time. The patent numbers cast into the combined exhaust/inlet manifold, numbers 162853, 119187, 9240 and 24316 all relate to improvements to carburettors.

Wolseley

once more to acquire his 'old' company two years later.

In October 1926 a creditor commenced proceedings against the company for the sum of £466-10s-0d and Sir Gilbert Garnsey and T.W. Horton were appointed as Joint Receivers and Managers, but on the 1st November the company was declared bankrupt with liabilities of over £2,000,000. This was a sad and catastrophic end to a company which had been amongst the earliest pioneers of the British motor car industry, had diversified into fields far greater than possibly any other British motor car company had attempted and had been the countries largest motor car company prior to the First World War. In 1903 Wolseley had produced 800 cars rising to 3,000 cars in 1913, almost 7% of the market when 44,000 cars had been produced in Britain. Its customers had included Royalty, Dukes, Earls, Lords, Maharajah's, Admirals and Generals and its products had been respected and admired the world over, but it had failed to cope with post war economic conditions and collapsed, not as a result of its own making one suspects, but as a direct result of Vickers insistance that Wolseley must buy the Drews Lane factory of the Electric & Ordnance Accessories Co.Ltd., which had put a noose around its neck. Had Wolseley not been shackled by this enforced acquisition and had been allowed to continue with their own expansion programme, and had difficulties then arisen allowed to contract back into the Adderley Park Works, even by selling off the Aero Site, the company would, in all probability, have weathered the economic storm and survived the Depression intact.

The Adderley Park works were capable of producing substantial numbers of vehicles as Morris Commercial were to prove in later years when they occupied the site and produced in excess of 50,000 vehicles per annum at the peak of production.

Vickers appear to have done nothing to rescue the company, although it was still heavily committed to the motor industry having converted the Crayford Works into a huge body building plant capable of producing 15,000 bodies per year.

When a motoring correspondent asked William Morris if he intended to put in a bid for Wolseley to secure the company's future he replied, "I just want half an hours quiet thinking over the matter before making up my mind". It is not known if he did just take half an hours thinking, but if he did it was to cost him £24,333 per minute as he bought the Wolseley company and all its assets in 1927 for £730,000 in cash, renamed the company Wolseley Motors (1927) Ltd., sacked the management and transferred all the car production to the Drews Lane factory. (Whilst the bidding for the company went on, Austin's Financial Director Mr E.L. Payton asked Morris how much further he was prepared to go with his bid and Morris replied "I am going just a bit further than you!" and so Austin's second attempt to regain his old company was rebuffed again by the actions of Morris). As well as Morris and Austin, a third bidder for the company, now generally accepted as General Motors of America also took part, confirming comments made earlier in this book that Wolseley products had aroused a great deal of interest just after the war.

Part of the East Works site (buildings 'b' and 'c') was sold to the S.U. Carburettor company where they remained until World War Two. Part of the Britannia Works, including the newly constructed 500 feet long four storey building, was sold to the Durex Abrasives company, which became part of the 3M's group. The South Works was also sold and, in 1929, the rest of the Adderley Park works was taken over by Morris Commercial Cars Ltd., as their Heavy Vehicle Works with the East Works site becoming a giant body building factory.

PHOTOGRAPHS

TOP: The 1922 "Wolseley" Ten 2 seater Coupe with fixed head, designed "to meet the need of clients who require a small closed carriage". This elegant little motor car cost £550.

CENTRE: The 1922 six cylinder 24/30 h.p. Touring Landaulette de Luxe based on a chassis with a wheelbase of 11ft 8ins with lowered sidemembers ahead of the rear axle to improve access to the rear passenger compartment. The side valve engine had a bore of 3.562" diameter, stroke of 5.5" and developed 60 b.h.p., driving through a four speed gearbox into a worm drive rear axle. The suspension featured normal semi-elliptics at the front and patented compensated cantilever springs to the rear. In chassis form alone the cost was £900 and the model shown in this photograph cost £1,450.

BOTTOM: Introduced in 1926 this 11/22 h.p. model featured a four cylinder overhead cam-shaft engine with all gear drive to the camshaft replacing the chain/gear combination of other Wolseley engines. With a bore of 2.562" diameter and stroke of 3.75" the engine was rated at 10.5 h.p. The car itself was based on a 8ft 9ins wheelbase chassis with a front track of 4ft 2ins, had a three speed gearbox and worm drive rear axle. The four seater shown here cost £235 and a two seater, plus Dickey for two more passengers, was also available at the same price.

WOLSELEY TOOL & MOTOR CAR COMPANY LIMITED
ADDERLEY PARK WORKS — 1912

BRITANNIA WORKS **WEST WORKS** **EAST WORKS**

REPAIR SHOPS

PLATING SHOP
RESERVOIR
EXPERIMENTAL SHOP

MARINE DEPT.
MACHINE SHOPS

BOARD ROOM
SALES OFFICE

ENGINE HOUSE
PAINT SHOP
MESS ROOMS

COACHSMITHS SHOP

LNWR RAILWAY

CHASSIS ERECTING SHOP

FORGING SHOP
ORIGINAL FOUNDRY CONVERTED TO MACHINE SHOPS

DRAWING OFFICE

REPAIR SHOP
CAR TEST TRACK

STORES
BOILER HOUSE
UPHOLSTERING AND PAINT SHOP

BRITANNIA WORKS **WEST WORKS** **EAST WORKS**

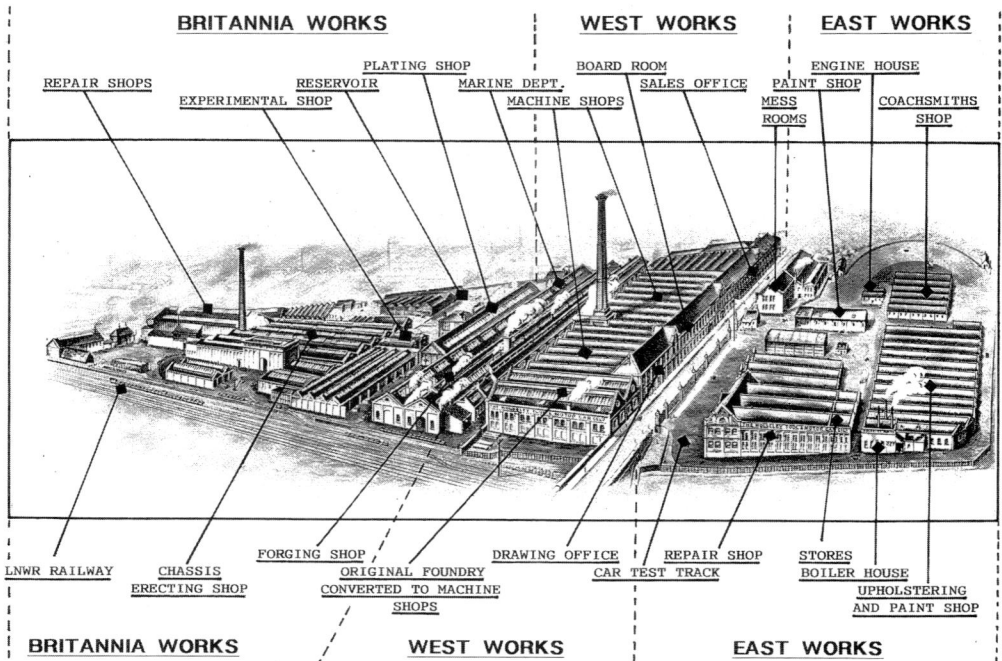

WOLSELEY MOTORS LIMITED
ADDERLEY PARK WORKS — 1914

REPAIR SHOPS
IRON FOUNDRY
ALUMINIUM FOUNDRY

SAWMILLS

ENGINE ERECTING SHOP

DRAWING OFFICE

CAR TEST SHED

BODY STORES
PAINT SHOP

WING SHOP

BODY MOUNTING
UPHOLSTERING SHOP

CHASSIS CONSTRUCTION SHOP

CARRIAGE SMITHS

BODY SHOP

MACHINE SHOPS

FINISHED TEST SHOP

DRIVING DEPT.
WINDOW FRAME MAKERS

VARNISHING SHOP

FINISHING SHOP

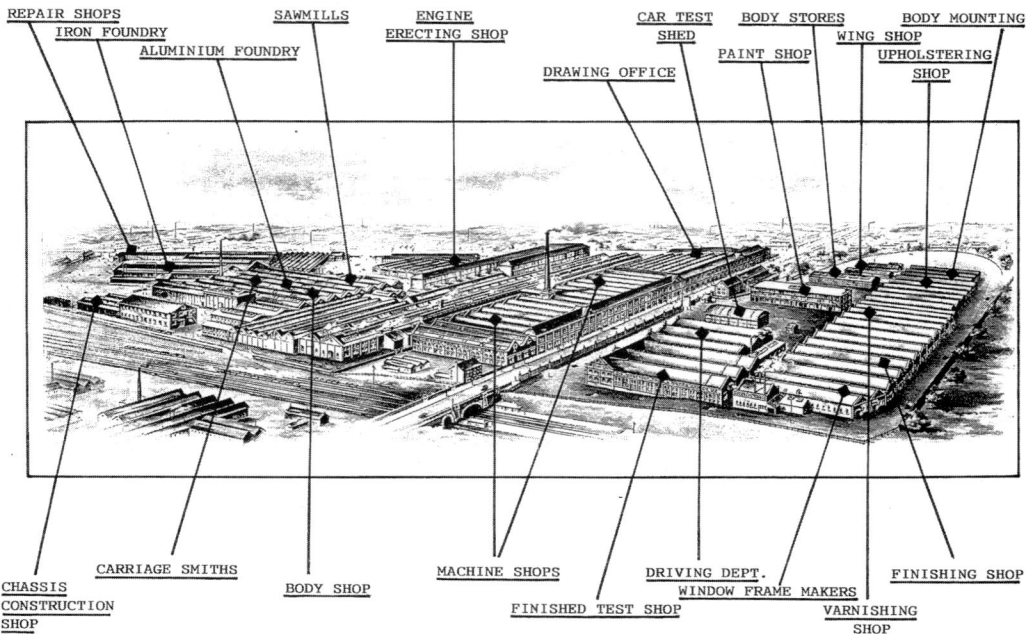

WOLSELEY MOTORS LIMITED
ADDERLEY PARK WORKS — 1918

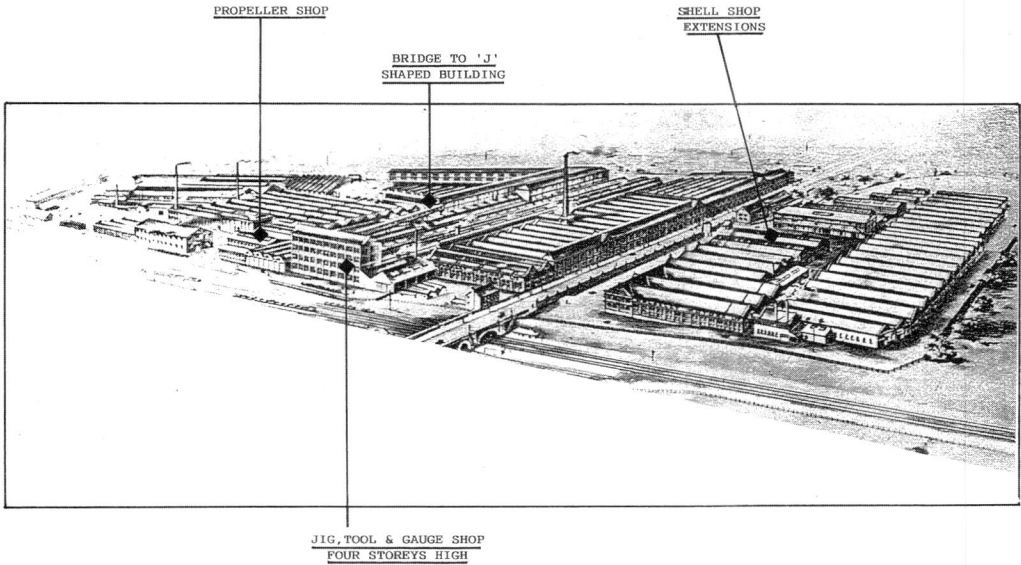

PROPELLER SHOP

BRIDGE TO 'J' SHAPED BUILDING

SHELL SHOP EXTENSIONS

JIG,TOOL & GAUGE SHOP FOUR STOREYS HIGH

WOLSELEY MOTORS LIMITED
ADDERLEY PARK WORKS & SOUTH WORKS — 1926

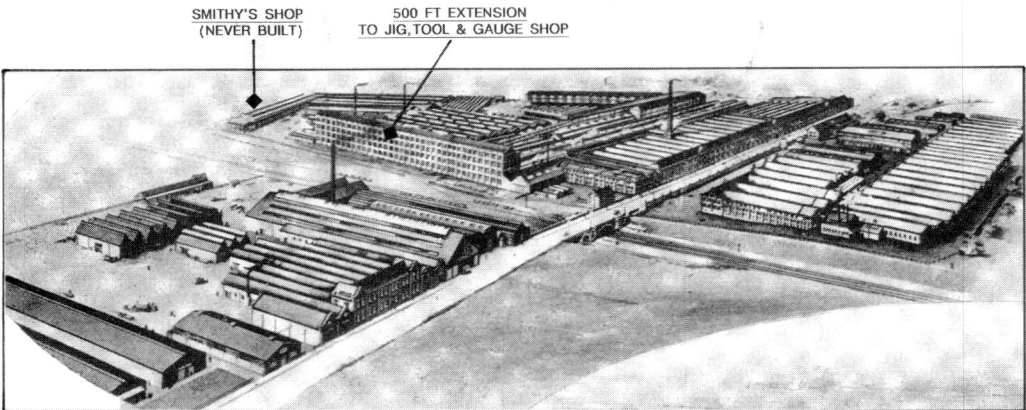

SMITHY'S SHOP (NEVER BUILT)

500 FT EXTENSION TO JIG,TOOL & GAUGE SHOP

NOTE:– This combined view of the Adderley Park Works and South Works appeared widely, in various forms, in Wolseley sales literature after the First World War but, unfortunately, it gives a totally misleading picture as to the relative positions of these two sites. From this picture it would appear that the South Works (left side of picture) was just across the railway bridge in Bordesley Green Road from the main Adderley Park Works, whereas in fact, this particular site was actually occupied by the Adderley Park Brick Works and the Wolseley South Works was about 250 yards south of the bridge and would have been well out of sight in this aerial view!!

INDEX